THE GAME BEFORE THE GAME

DARRIUS "DEE" OLDHAM

The Game Before the Game

Copyright © 2022 by Darrius "Dee" Oldham
ISBN: 979-8-218-00059-2

Oldham Tour Enterprise, LLC | DOTS Logistics, LLC
944 Jefferson Street, Nashville, TN 37208

www.OldhamTour.org

CONTENTS

1. Dreams and Nightmares 1
2. Connecting the Dots 9
3. The Black Sheep 23
4. Thin Ice 35
5. Better Man 45
6. Mamba Mentality 63
7. Visitation Room 83
8. Tunnel Vision 101
9. Toxic Smile 115
10. Respect the Game 129

1
DREAMS AND NIGHTMARES

I always walked down the starting lineup tunnel. I never ran. That was my swag. They would say my name and it's just like, "This is my time." I was the fourth player called to the court and I would pass through a tunnel of my teammates, with their arms held out as we all listened to the crowd screaming. Some cheerleaders would be part of the tunnel, with the others on the sidelines flipping and doing all kinds of stuff. If it was a big game, you'd have some of the student section in the tunnel – and we had a huge student section at Wilson Central.

I would walk down that tunnel with both hands out, stretch them all the way out. I imagine it's like a red-carpet experience. It's my moment. I would get to the end and give the last guy a handshake. I had my little signature thing where I would put my hands up and a team member would start patting me down like I'm trying to get through security claims. Then I'd go around to the opposing coach, acknowledge him with a first bump, and come back into the team huddle, ready to play.

That energy in the room always makes you feel like the man of the year. Hearing the roar of a crowd is a huge adrenaline rush. In that high school gym, in college, in the pros, that never gets old. It's like, "Bring it on! Bring it on!" It helps me perform. If it's a big crowd, I'm going to show out. The more people, the more you can expect from me. Like, "Let's go, let's lock in."

I'm going to be a little arrogant right here. I was good. I was very exceptional at basketball, especially for where I lived. Eventually, people around Lebanon, Tennessee, started coming to the games just to see me play. Word started getting out around like, "You got to get up there and see that kid at Wilson Central." When we played our rivals, the gym would be swamped. Sometimes when we were getting ready to run out as a team for warmups, you might hear somebody over the rail, like, "Let's go, boy! Let's go! It's time!" Or I would hear a family member yelling, especially at big games.

I tell you what, no matter if there's a million people in that gym, and this was the same way in college, I can always pick out mom's voice. Even if everybody's screaming, I can hear that voice in the distance. No matter how many people are in that gym, I can hear her as if there's nobody there. When that woman gets to screaming, I can hear it! It doesn't matter what's going on, whether she's screaming at me or the referee. It's going to be one or the other. Most times she'd be screaming at me or telling me to rebound or shoot the ball, shouting, "Wake up! Come on, man, get the ball!" I remember when we played the University of Georgia in my senior year of college. They have a pretty big arena and she was sitting up top, a good ways away, and I knew exactly where she was sitting because I could hear her. She was going to be heard.

My problem was always my mindset. I was so broken on the inside. It messed with my confidence. There was never a question of, was I able? Or was I talented enough? Maybe I didn't necessarily believe that I could do it. When you go through what I went through as a kid, it's common to feel like everybody can see that on you. As I walked onto the court, I would think that people could look at me and tell that I lived in a one-bedroom house and that my father was in prison. It's like I had a sign on my head.

Even with my athletic achievements, there was a voice inside me saying, "Who do you think you are?" And another voice saying, "This is too much for you. This ain't where you're supposed to be. You're a kid from a broken home. You don't belong in this room. Yeah, you got to do your thing on the court, but boy, you're poor and your clothes are raggedy." It was a lack of confidence that I was dealing with. It caused me to not believe in myself and caused me to often second-guess myself. It caused me to always need reassurance when in reality I was the most gifted kid out there. Everybody could see that but me. I would show flashes of it. I would tap in and every now and again have a breakout night and score thirty points, but then I might give you a game where I score eight.

I couldn't quite put it all together back then but going into those tunnels before the game felt like a high. There used to be a Beats commercial where Colin Kaepernick is walking through a tunnel and everybody beside him is screaming, just going nuts about him. The song in the background is "I'm The Man." He has the headphones on and he is tuning out everything. That's kind of what it feels like: "Look at me."

If not controlled properly, that attention can take you off the deep end too, because you start feeling above and privileged. You can lose a sense of reality and human connection. You might mistreat people, thinking you're better than people, if you're not careful. Later on, that started to play a little bit on my relationship with my mother. When I got my full ride to college, as I started to elevate and grow more as a person, it was hard for me to really find respect for ones who I felt hadn't done much. I was allowing accolades and achievements to describe a person's worth. And that ain't how it works at all.

January 14, 2011. I was a junior in high school and riding in the car with my mom, coming back home after winning a road game at Portland High School. That night, I was trying to convince my mom to let me go out and celebrate the victory with my brother. Whenever I had the time, I would always try to hang out with my him. We're four years apart. I was 16 at the time and he'd just dropped out of college.

From birth to adulthood, my brother and I spent every day together, through the entire struggle. He was the first consistent male figure in my life, period. An older male influence who was a protector, a voice of reasoning, and simply just my big brother. He paved the way for me in athletics because he was a beast at football. I didn't have a dad at home, so everything was about my big brother, walking behind him. College was not something we were familiar with as a family. He started getting recruited by Division I colleges for his football ability, taking visits to colleges, and opening up our eyes to a completely different life.

He went to Wilson Central before I got there. They knew I was coming in as a little brother when my big brother was doing his thing. It gave me a little bit of leverage. Like, "Let's see what his little brother's got. Let's give him a chance." He was the first one to walk through that door and establish a name for himself. When I came in, he had cleared out some of the static.

I was hoping he was going to wait on me to get home after the game, so I could get in the car with him and his friends before they headed out. However, I had a game the next day in Shelbyville, Tennessee. My mom was like, "You ain't going out. It's already 10:30, 11:00. You know you got to be in by midnight and you got a game tomorrow. No."

Me being me, I'm trying to wheel and deal. I'm agitated because I'm not getting my way. I was rebellious and she was doing her best to keep grips on me. I was slowly transitioning into that kid who has all the answers, who knows everything. I'm like, "I'm going to be up in time." I knew I could get to school that next morning in time for walkthrough. On the way home that night, I'm pissed off. I'm done talking for the rest of the car ride, just looking out the window. But by the time we get home, everything felt back to normal. Get me some dinner, get into bed, get me some rest and be ready for tomorrow.

I woke up early the next morning to my grandmother screaming. It was barely daylight outside, probably about 6:30 or 7:00. Her room was on the other side of the house, but by the noise alone, you would have thought she was right next to me. We all lived together—me, my mom, my grandma and my brother—and I figured something was going on because suddenly I realized we had other family at the house. I could see my aunt standing by my bed, crying. Now I know something's wrong, but I don't know what. All she was saying was, "Your brother... your brother...." Finally, she said, "He got in a car wreck this morning."

She then told me that my brother, who had been driving that night, got rushed to the hospital. One of his friends in the wreck got life-flighted to Vanderbilt and the other one was dead on the scene. I shouted, "Where's my mama?" and my aunt said, "She's up there now to go see about it." She thought they would take my brother in to jail or custody, after they figured out if he was OK. We knew he was facing severe charges and that my mom had to scramble up $20,000 to bail him out. At the time we didn't know if alcohol was related. Did he fall asleep, did someone hit them, or what? We were obviously praying for the best but preparing for the worst.

As soon as that morning news cranks up at 5 or 6, it's on there. My aunt asked me, "Do you still want to go to your game in Shelbyville?" In my mind, I was indecisive. I wanted to be there for my brother, but at the same time I knew he would expect me to go to my game, so that's what I did. When I got to school for walkthrough, it's like I'm walking in with a huge red light over my body. Everybody's looking at me, wanting to ask, but also thinking, "I don't know if we should ask." I could feel it as soon as I walked in the door. It's always a chattery room, but as soon as I walked in, it got stiff and quiet. I'm feeling it. I haven't done anything, but they know this is my brother. They know what I'm going through.

The coach called the whole team to the huddle and broke the ice. "We all are aware there's a lot going on," he said. "I can only imagine what Dee has seen this morning. We're not going to be interrogating or asking questions. We're just going to support and be there for him and go win this basketball game." But my closest friends would still ask, "What happened?"

That day at Shelbyville, my mind was everywhere except for that damn game. I had to force my mental fortitude to play but I wasn't myself. I was checked out. I still played fairly decent, but I wasn't Dee. On the bus ride to the game, I was able to talk to my brother on the phone because my mom bailed him out that morning. I was able to hear his voice, but he sounded out of it. I don't think he had processed what had happened.

After the game, I just wanted to get back home and see my brother. I wanted to lay my eyes on him. The family was over at the house too, and I could tell it still hadn't registered with my brother what had happened. One of the most heart-tugging things was seeing him go through this transition, seeing him deal and battle with that as a young adult, knowing that this was an accident. He made a mistake that he had to pay for. The reports ended up coming back and stated that one too many drinks were consumed, so it ended in my brother serving time in jail and placed on probation for eight years upon release. I mean, hell, that's almost his entire 20s.

While all of this was going on, my dad was in the prison system serving 262 months. You do the math: About 21 years. My dad and his brother both have served over 20 years in the prison system. They've been incarcerated more than one time and they've had lengthy sentences. My uncle received two life sentences. My granddad—my dad's dad—went in first. He did sixteen and a half years in prison. I do know that some of his other kids have done prison time, but I've only met them in passing and haven't been able to form a good relationship with them.

My brother and I have separate dads. His dad was probably the most consistent male through all this time. He was around often when we were growing up, but he served some jail time for petty stuff or small misdemeanors. He was in and out of our lives because he and my mom were in an ongoing relationship from when she was 16 to her early 20s.

When I think about my childhood and the things I was into, I was basically that curious kid that wasn't afraid to jump off the porch. My brother was the polar opposite. He was very introverted, quiet, never in trouble, never got an in-school suspension. Just the last person you would expect to be put in handcuffs, let's put it that way. It blew everybody's mind, like, "I can't even picture this guy sitting in a jail system." It doesn't even go together.

The way that my brother was perceived when the accident happened was just absurd… I don't think his friends supported him how they should have. They almost distanced themselves from him as if he was a serial killer or something, if that makes sense. This could have happened to anybody. We've all had nights where we'd go out, hang out, probably have a few more drinks than we should, and think, "I can make it home." Before you know it, that quick, the trajectory of your life changes drastically.

For a while I thought, "Damn, I was supposed to be with them." It didn't stick with me for too long, but I do remember that crossing my mind. Then I thought, had I been there, that accident wouldn't have happened. I could have prevented it. My mom really saved me from getting caught up in the mix.

We attended the funeral of the young man who lost his life in the car accident and you could feel all the eyes in the room on us as we walked in. We came in as a family, but I can't imagine how that felt for my brother, listening to all the personal stories from the people who were speaking and seeing all the tears. I can't even imagine the amount of blame, shame, and many other emotions that my brother, my first hero, experienced during that time as a 20-year-old young man just getting started with life.

The night of the accident, it started out with four of them – three guys and a girl. They were in her car and she was the driver initially. On the way to the club, around 11 that night, they got pulled over. She had warrants for her arrest—failure to appear or something like that. So, she got arrested and the cops asked my brother and his friends if any of them had a valid driver's license. They did, so the police officer turned the vehicle over to them, and told them to go ahead and go wherever they were going after he had to take her in. It was one of those situations that put you in the place of a man trying to help and then it turns out sour. They were all out having a night of fun and my brother felt he was the most equipped to get them home safely. But the people at the funeral would never know the back story. All they're looking at is that a drunk driver killed somebody.

Watching all of this happen in my family ignited a fire in me to really do the opposite, because at this point, you ain't got no choice but to do right. If I don't do this for nobody else, I've got to do this for my family. I decided that I'm going to rebrand this family, because at that time it felt like we were just a black hole.

2
CONNECTING THE DOTS

Everybody in our family came to the hospital, taking up the whole waiting room. Waiting on me. My mom had been in labor for 22 hours. She didn't end up having any complications. I just wasn't ready.

Right after I was born, a week late, they cleaned me up and put me in the nursery with all these white babies, neatly lined up right by the window. Now, in my family, if one person goes to the hospital, we all go. It's a social event. Somebody in our family lifted up my brother, who was just 3 years old at the time, and put his nose to the glass as my mother and I were brought to the window. Somebody told him, "That's your little brother."

And he said, "I don't want that black one."

We all still laugh about that. Because it did take me so long to arrive, my grandmother thought I was bruised. After a couple of weeks, my skin did lighten but I was still dark. In our family, we're all fair-skinned, so this was a surprise to everyone. When we'd go places, strangers would do a double take. At the ballpark with my brother, people would watch us play together. They'd say to my mother, "I thought you had two kids." She'd say, "I do. They're over there playing." And they would be like, "Oh, that one's yours?"

My parents met in high school through a mutual friend. As teenagers, they would all pile into the car and go into Nashville, hanging out together like kids do now. They'd go to skating parties out by Rivergate Mall, things like that. After my dad graduated and went off to college, he would come home on the weekends and she would meet him in Nashville. They'd spend the weekend together, having fun. Basically, one thing led to another and that's I came along, but they weren't boyfriend and girlfriend.

When I arrived in the world on May 3, 1994, it scared my mom to death. Along with playing football on scholarship, my dad was pursuing a degree in physics at Kentucky Wesleyan College in Owensboro. He wasn't at the hospital because there was some kind of question, in his opinion, if I was even his child. So, he sent his mom to come to the hospital for clarity while he was taking exams during finals week. And once she lays eyes at me, she obviously knows there is no way around it. My mom calls in the nurse to show me to my dad's mom. First, my grandma says, "Oh." That's all she says. She goes outside and calls my dad, telling him, "Oh no, there's no denying this. Spitting image. He's yours. There's no doubt about it."

My dad didn't know about me until my mom was four months pregnant. She says now that she couldn't come to grips with it herself. She was 23 years old and already had a 3-year-old that she'd just gotten potty-trained. When the doctor told her she was pregnant again, her immediate response was, "No, I can't have another baby. I just got the hang of this." When she finally told my dad, he responded, "You must be kidding me." From the day she told him about me, my parents quit speaking until she gave birth.

Soon after, my mom asked him to come home and do the proper paperwork. He said he wouldn't leave school because of finals. She told him, "OK, if you don't sign the birth certificate, he cannot go into your name. He'll be in my name." Well, he didn't come home. In my teens, I used to dwell on that for so long, especially when I was dealing with those insecurities and those traumatic feelings. I used to always think back to, like, this fool wasn't even there when I was born. That's why I don't have his last name. I have my mom's last name.

Also, Dad was living a double life. When he was with my mom, she didn't know anything about this other lifestyle he had. Not at all. When he went back to Owensboro, he had a whole other family there. My mom only found out about them when she got pregnant with me because his new girlfriend started calling. His girlfriend said my mom must have picked my dad's name out of a hat and that he wasn't her baby daddy. He always had this other woman barking in his ear, telling him, "No, that baby probably isn't yours."

After coming home from the hospital, it was my mom, my brother, and me. The community we grew up in is called LaGuardo, Tennessee. It's in Wilson County, between Lebanon and Gallatin, off Highway 109. It's a very small, family-oriented town where the majority of the people know each other. We lived in a two-bedroom house, with a room on each end, but we used one like a storage room. We all slept in the same bed and I slept in the middle. We had one full bathroom and the other just had a shower. Laundry room. Living room. We had a table in the kitchen but we never ate dinner there. You'd just grab your plate and go back to where you were. We stayed warm in the winter by keeping the oven door open, letting the heat circulate throughout the house. Now that I think about it, that house was little as hell.

My great-grandparents had thirteen girls and four boys. They lived in LaGuardo when they were having all these children. My great-grandmother thought something was up with me because I didn't talk much until I was almost 3 years old. She would say that I was just taking it all in, or that I wasn't talking yet because I was too busy studying people. But when I finally started talking, I never stopped. She was a social butterfly too. That's where I get that quality. Her friends would call and she'd have me sing to them over the telephone. She thought I was the grandest thing after I started talking. She died when I was 3 and I sang "I Believe I Can Fly" at her funeral.

My mom's mom has always lived in the same area. Granny never legally got married but she was in a long-term relationship with a man that I would consider my grandfather. Pork Chop was a veteran and a very wealthy man in the town, a full-fledged entrepreneur. When he got out of the service, he had a lot of things going on. Had dump trucks running on the road, had between four to seven houses in LaGuardo to rent out. He was a very, very business-savvy individual.

Mom was never married through any of these times. She made up her mind to make her kids her number one priority. As far back as I can remember, my mother has worked two jobs minimum. She started working part-time at Kroger when she was 16. When she found out she was pregnant with my brother, she had to drop out of a nursing program at Vol State. She worked 30 years at Kroger, started off bagging groceries, but ended up becoming a pharmacist technician. She's also a licensed cosmetologist. To provide, that's always been her drive.

I was the class clown from the beginning, the center of attention. The funny part about it is, I've always been a likable guy. I never was a guy that walked around feeling like lonely. People gravitated toward me although I wasn't really sure why. Like, what is it that you like about me?

In first grade, I kissed a girl in our classroom and word got out. I can't remember exactly how it was worded, but it was made clear that her dad would be highly upset if he found out his daughter was kissing a black boy. Her mom worked at the school. Believe it or not, her mom was one of those moms. She wanted to be the cool mom, where it's about being friends with her kids instead of being a parent. The girl came back in class crying because her mom had just got on her ass. It wasn't even really about the kissing; it was the fact of who she kissed. Her mom told the girl, "You don't do that." It ended up circling back to me that she's not allowed to talk to black boys. I'll never forget that.

However, I can't remember when the black jokes started. A lot of them started coming from older peers, older guys, like my brother's friends. It'd be from black people joking about me for being dark. Someone would turn out the light and say, "Where's Dee?" I would just laugh and go along with it. Looking back, it built a sense of humor and it built character. Sports became my way of dealing with things like that. I looked at my situation and realized that people were going to accept me because I was good at something.

I played baseball and football before I started playing basketball. I would play basketball on the blacktop at school during recess and every day at Kids Club before my mom picked me up. When I heard about the tryouts for a league at West Elementary, I was like, "Dang, I kind of want to try this." After getting in the car, I told my mom about it. She asked, "When are the tryouts?" I said, "Tonight." She said, "Tonight? And you're only just now telling me about it?"

My mom didn't even think I knew how to dribble but she took me there anyway. She wanted me to prove it to her, to see it for herself. All these kids ran onto the court and I'm easily the tallest one in my age group, much taller than anyone else. From the bleachers, my mom watched me shooting the ball and doing layups with ease and she could not believe it. Before long, one of the other coaches from the older team came up to her and said, "This boy is a natural! Where did he learn that from?" She's tripping, like, "I don't know!" Then everybody's coming up to her after the tryouts and she's feeling proud, but she's telling them, "I didn't even know he could play!"

Within my first or second year on that league, a man in a leather coat who looked about seven feet tall approached my mother after a game at Southside Elementary in Lebanon, where he coached. He introduced himself as Coach Gary and asked, "Are you Darrius' mother?" Her immediate thought was, "Oh God, what did he do now." Instead, Coach Gary asked if I would be interested in playing in AAU, which stands for Amateur Athletic Union, a youth travel basketball circuit. Every summer, a collective group of kids would be put together and play on the weekends in different tournaments.

My mom and I didn't know what he was talking about. Like, "You mean travel to different cities and states to play basketball?" We didn't have any money, so my mom's already wondering how we're going to do this. Of course, she wasn't going to say that to him because she's the kind of person who may not have a penny to her name, but she's not going to let you know. Coach Gary said, "I tell you what, y'all come to a practice on Sunday and give it a feel. We'll go from there."

I was always an athlete. I could run and jump but I wasn't very skilled. When I walked into the gym on that first day, the whole team was already picked but they were looking for a couple more guys. Coach Gary had explained to us that he'd been hearing about my ability on the court, and that he wanted me to be on the team, but first he needed to know if I would fit in with the other kids. In other words, he didn't want just anybody coming in. There needed to be chemistry. So, I basically practiced with them. They were doing left-handed layups and I could tell they had been doing this for a little while. It was a 10-and-under team and I was 9. And I was the only black dude.

I was nervous because it was unfamiliar, but I'm a competitor by nature. I've always been in "survival of the fittest" situations to where we got to make it happen ourselves.

We spent about two hours that day at the rec center in Lebanon, with my mom watching from the stands. After practice, riding home in the car, I told her all about everybody I just met. Where they went to school, who their sister was, where they lived. She must have been thinking, "How did you get all that information from these people when you just met them?" Not long after that, Coach Gary called her and said that I fit in perfectly. He wanted me to be part of the team. She told him, "We don't have a problem playing, but financially, we just can't do this."

He said, "Well, I tell you what I'm going to do. We get sponsors for this team. The uniforms, the shoes, everything will be paid for, and if there's money left, they will pay for anything else that we need. But right now, we're going to start off local." It wasn't long, though, before we were killing all the local teams in these tournaments and the coaches wanted to us to play out of town. Nine times out of ten, sponsors would pay for everything. We didn't have to come out of pocket. That was the only way we could do it.

I ended up playing with that team for four years and change. Still got good relationships with those guys to this day. However, this team was all white. Not all of the guys on my team were rich but most of their parents had good jobs. A majority of them had two-parent households. They had a close-knit community group, just a real family-oriented program, which is what I needed as well.

This is when my underprivileged lifestyle really came into the scene. The coach might say, "We're going to be getting changed in the locker room before the game." I'm like, "What? We got locker rooms?" I'm thinking that's such a big deal. I'm so used to getting changed in the car, walking in, playing the game, and leaving. Now we're going to have shooting shirts, like pullovers and jumpsuits, to do warm-ups? This is NBA stuff. That opened my mind to a whole other realm.

Every time we would go out of town for a game, the team would stay at an extended-stay hotel or somewhere with a kitchen. Mom would go to the grocery store before we left and the three of us would eat our dinner in the room. Spaghetti, chips, drinks, sandwich meat, all that. We kept it all in coolers with ice packs. My brother didn't really care one way or the other because he didn't eat much anyway, but I would get upset that we couldn't go out to eat. But we knew that when it came time to eat, we better not act a fool and say anything out of the ordinary to make anyone think we didn't have money. My mom didn't want to be a charity case, but she would purchase food stamps from friends before we left. She could make those groceries last all weekend long. Nobody needed to know we were one paycheck from the poor house.

Basically, you just didn't talk about it. Even though they knew why we were eating in our room, nobody said a word. Nobody ever made any remarks. A lot of the kids wished they could stay in the room with us and eat our food because they didn't want to go out with their parents. They weren't going to McDonald's, where maybe we could go. They'd go to Longhorn or Outback. Then when they got back to the hotel, I'd go meet the kids at the pool. We never did go hungry.

Our AAU coach, Mark Thompson, explains it to this day how he just knew at that time that I had a gift. He says he knew immediately that I was a hard worker, that I didn't mind working. He also recognized that I had a good mother who was raising me right. Most importantly, he said, "You came from a good foundation, a foundation of principal." And that's the thing. He could see that, but in my mind, I couldn't.

The first time my dad went to jail, I was 10 months old. He spent 30 days locked up. Then, sixteen months later, he went back in for a three-year term. By the time he got out in September 1999, I was 5 years old. By Christmas of 2001, he was back in jail. Because I was still young, I don't remember much about those times, but my cousins and I would go visit him in Grayson County, Kentucky. Then on the back end of his time, he was at a halfway house, so my grandma would take food in and we'd have family time. When he got out in January 2004, he would travel back and forth from Kentucky on the weekends to come see me, so that I'd get a few short stints with him, but it had rarely been full-fledged father-son time. I can count on one hand how many times that happened, where it was just me and him.

Instead, he would buy me things. Keeping me in new shoes, keeping me in new clothes. I would be so thrilled when I knew I was going somewhere with him. He had a big Suburban with speakers in the back, spotless rims, and TVs in the back of the seats. Seeing him was my escape from reality. I was living the high life when I was with him because he's having all this money. He had the loud flashy things, nice clothes, nice cars, and always had new shoes. I wasn't having that living with my mom. I would always say things to trigger her, like, "When I get old, I'm going to live with my dad." Or, "I'm going to be like my daddy." As a child, that's what had my attention—shiny and glittery—not understanding that you don't want that life at all. But as a child looking at the struggle versus looking like he's got it going on, that's what my mind was attracted to.

I'll never forget, I was in fourth grade and I knew that my dad was getting out this day at a specific time. The whole day, I'm not even focused on school. I'm looking at the clock. By this time, my dad's mother had given me my first cell phone, which my mom was very upset about. Because I didn't have a chance to spend much time with my dad's mom, she would spoil me when she saw me. I loved it! She would give me money or shoes, something like that, and then she gave me a Nokia with an antenna that you'd pull up. I still remember my number: 389-8742.

There was more to it, though. Before that, when my dad wanted to call me, he'd have to call my mom's number. So, his mother and his new wife wanted me to have my own phone so he could get directly to me without going through my mom. He didn't want to have to fight and argue every time he wanted to talk to his son. And every time he called me, he had to argue with her because she wanted to know why he was calling me. That's why his mother gave me that phone.

Mom kept a tight knit on my brother and me. We didn't get out of sight. And if we did, we had to have a real good lie. Then two or three days later, she knew about it. We couldn't hide anything too easily because she was always in our business and she didn't care. To this day, she says I didn't need to be walking around with a darn cell phone when I was 8 years old. But because of my low confidence, anything where I could be one step ahead of somebody, or have something up on somebody, it helped my self-esteem.

Anyway, I couldn't wait to get out of school that day so I could call him. To be able to call him on a cell phone! I had never done that before. As soon as that bell rang, I called him up in Kentucky after my grandma had given me his cell number and I was like, "What you doing?" And he was like, "Man, sitting at the table eating a big bowl of spaghetti." I don't know what it was about that moment, but that was a surreal feeling, being able to have that experience. Very small, but it meant so much.

A few months later, he picked me up in Nashville and we went on a road trip back up to Kentucky. He was driving a Buick and "Go DJ" by Lil Wayne came on the radio. That was my dad's favorite song and every time it came on, we'd just be singing it together. I'm riding in the front seat as a little boy and I'm sure he's seeing himself in the flesh, looking over at me. That's what made that memory so vivid. It was a special bonding moment that I'll never forget.

He drove to his friend's house and his friend had a son who was my age. I forget the boy's name. His dad said, "Why don't y'all go outside and play for a little bit?" So, we go shoot some ball, play with the dogs. We were out there probably 10 minutes. Then I'm trying to go back inside and the door is locked. I'm knocking and nobody comes. Like, where's everybody? Eventually I stopped knocking and went back to shoot basketball.

Finally, the kid's dad comes to the door and we go back in. From the living room, where I decided to sit and watch TV, you could see the kitchen table, where my dad is having something to eat. Before too long, another one of their friends comes into the kitchen. This guy says, "I got this much left," and as he's saying it, he's glancing over his shoulder into the living room to see if I'm looking. So they did what they did, with my dad acting like he ain't even involved.

After that, Dad and I ended up leaving that place. Then we made another stop at some abandoned home where a guy happened to be inside playing video games. That's what they call a trap house. At the time, I didn't know that we were on a drug deal.

And it wasn't probably even a year after that when he went back to prison.

That's when my heart really shattered. It happened in April 2005, when I was 10 years old. I was in Tullahoma, Tennessee, at an AAU tournament and he was supposed to be coming down there that weekend to watch me play. I had been calling his phone all day and I wasn't getting an answer. That wasn't like him to not answer or call back. After the game, back at the hotel, I was like, "Mom, did my daddy try to call you or anything?" She's like, "No, I ain't heard from him."

It's nighttime at this point. I called the house phone where he and his wife lived. At this time, she was pregnant and I had my first sister on the way. I'm like, "Hey, Carolyn, is my dad there? I've been trying to call him. Have you heard from my daddy?" She didn't say nothing. I'm like, "Hello?" I can tell she's crying. She says, "I think you need to call your grandmother and talk to her about it." That's all she said.

Mind you, Granny hadn't called me. Because if something had happened, you would think that somebody would notify us. I said, "OK." I hung up and called my grandma immediately. I said, "Granny, what's Carolyn talking about? I just called looking for my dad and she's crying. What's going on?" Granny took a deep breath and this is exactly what she said: "Well, he's back in jail."

She didn't really explain descriptively what had happened, but it was just like the world stopped, just... BOOM! I still remember my mom's response. She wasn't boo-hooing, but it was just like silent tears. I don't know if she felt for me or if it was one of them deals where it's like, damn, I really got to raise this boy on my own.

I ended up getting the whole story about why he got arrested. My dad was supposed to be meeting a guy at a gas station somewhere in Kentucky for a transaction. Dad showed up and the guy was late. Red flag number one. Dad called the guy and he ain't answering the phone. So eventually the guy called back and he's like, "I'm over here at McDonald's across the street." Why are you changing location? Another red flag. Right after Dad pulled up into the parking lot, the guy blocked his car by parking behind him. Then, Dad went and sat in the guy's car for a brief time. After being shown the drugs, Dad got back out of the car to get the money. Instantly, a swarm of officers jumped out of the bushes with guns pointed. He dropped down on the asphalt, right there in the McDonald's parking lot, and one of the officers pressed a knee into his back. Across the street, my dad noticed an older lady on her porch. Suddenly she stood up and yelled, "Don't y'all hurt that man!" From that day forward, he's been locked up.

Not long after that arrest, he wrote me a letter. That was the first form of communication we had since he went back to jail, and in that letter he explained that one of the reasons he was trying to sell those drugs was to earn some money to buy me a dirt bike for my birthday. It was almost like a guilt trip. At that time, I'm like, "What the hell do you mean? YOU did this. I could live without a dirt bike if this is what you had to do to get it."

When my mom found out that he got busted with over a hundred thousand dollars and we're down here living in poverty, she was pissed. We didn't even know he was that big in the game. He put us all in danger by living a double life, coming back and forth trafficking. He lived away from us, so we didn't know what he was doing day to day. We didn't have any other choice but to believe what he told us. He was making all this money and he wasn't taking care of his child. He lived this big-time lifestyle and we're down here struggling.

My dad would throw my mom some money every now and then, like when the car needed new tires because we were traveling so much. But in her mind, time is worth more than money. Money comes and goes. Those memories, you can't get them back. She felt like she'd come this far without him and she could do the rest without him too. It was nothing for her to leave him high and dry. All she had to do was not answer the phone. When I told her about the dirt bike blame, she said, "You tell him to call me when you talk to him next."

The next time he called, I handed my mother the phone, she told him, "Don't you ever tell my child that you did this to get a birthday present for him. You did this for yourself. You've always done this for yourself. It's all about you all the time and this materialistic shit that you can live without. We're doing fine without it. And if you ever tell my child that the reason why you did it is because of him, if you ever let something else like that come out your mouth, you'll never see him again."

That entire situation was another thing that I held on to for a while. To me, it just screams lack of accountability and it's like, "This ain't nobody's fault but yours. You woke up and chose this." That was another layer of the disappointment I had in him that added to my traumatic ways of thinking. Something that small. It's crazy how little things can have such a huge impact. That's when I started experiencing a shift. I had a lot of anger and unanswered questions pent up in me. Second thoughts, second guesses, just feeling sorry for myself and mad at the world.

When I started AAU, I barely knew the basics. I couldn't even make a left-hand layup or dribble on my offhand. I had no knowledge of that, but AAU taught me. That is when discipline first was instilled in me because I had a coach who did not play around. Coach Mark Thompson, who didn't even have a kid on the team. He'd get in my face during the game but he'd give me a hug afterwards. I love him to this day. He could get the best out of me when nobody else could. We still stay in touch as adults. But he has zero tolerance for lack of effort. He can work with you not being the most skilled. He can work with you not being the most talented. But you are going to work hard.

I always tell people, "Hard work beats talent when talent don't work hard." Our team would go to these tournaments and hold our own and had mad respect. No matter what it is you're going up against, Coach Mark's whole thing was, it don't matter what the situation is. You apply yourself. You put your best foot forward and give it everything you got. That's in anything in life. That was our foundation.

Coach Mark used to push us to the point to where you hated the guy, but it instilled discipline and hard work early. That's what made our team so good. We were very close and we worked hard. We played in Memphis every year and Memphis had these rough and rugged teams. You know, all-black teams. Memphis is a much rougher culture than Lebanon and here we are walking into their gym, white guys, parents all white. And one black guy. They're looking at us like, "Oh, we're going to kill these guys." In athletics that's the norm. That's the perspective of sports. You know, African Americans think white people can't play when it comes to basketball, when it comes to competing with athletic ability. Don't get it twisted. You got white people that do play football, whatever, but the stereotype is that they can't play. When we used to walk in gyms, people counted us out before the game even started. Then we would beat these teams because we had discipline.

Our team won a lot of tournaments. And every time we did, they'd put our black-and-white picture in the Lebanon newspaper. You'd see our white jerseys, hardly see my face, and then nine other white guys around me. I was outnumbered. It is literally like a speck because the rest of the team was white. That was stuff that played on my mind. It created so much insecurity, like I'm a black sheep. I'm just so different from everybody else. I'm so different from our society. I'm seeing all these children with their dads at school. I'm seeing dads and moms come to parent-teacher conferences. These are just experiences that I didn't have. I didn't even have a stepdad that stepped in to potentially implement this role of a male. At home it was just my mom, my grandma, and my brother.

That's when I can recall starting to seek male approval because it was nowhere to be found. Unfortunately, it was always from white men. All my teachers were white. Every sport I played, my coach was white. As a young black man, that can train your mind to think that white people are superior, because throughout my life, they were always in a place of prestige. Naturally, based on that environment, you just feel inferior about your own ethnicity. I would be constantly reminded that I'm different. I would look at my situation of my father being incarcerated and never around, and Mom doing the best she can. These were all just confirmations of what I was already struggling with. This is just confirming that I am different, that I ain't worth a damn.

The biggest thing that drew my attention back then was travel ball because it took me out of my environment. It gave me an escape from my reality. I'm getting to see things that I wouldn't get to see if I wasn't on that team. That alone increased my interest in the sport. I'm like, "You mean people are going around state to state and playing ball?" That kept me locked in. I was a hard worker. I was a good defender, but I didn't have exceptional skill that put me beyond other guys. That wasn't my role on that team because we had some guys at that age, at that competition level, who could play.

This is where the love of basketball really started to create because now here starts to come that recognition, that male acknowledgment, that I lacked and that I craved so much. Because I'm playing travel ball, it's like, "OK, I'm somebody." It gave me an identity. I got people other than my mom telling me how good I am at something. I looked forward to going to practices and traveling to games. We're going to Memphis, we're going to Orlando, we're going to Kentucky, we're going to all these places. Where I'm from, we ain't got the money to do that. And I'm doing something that I'm actually not bad at. That's when it started to cook on the inside, like, "OK, OK. I can do this."

3

THE BLACK SHEEP

In elementary school, we had the lunch line. What they serve, you get. Or you bring your lunch. At West Wilson Middle School, we had a cafeteria with so much more variety. You got a pizza line, you got a taco line, you got the little store area where you could pick something out. Depending on what day it is, they might have popcorn chicken, cheese sticks, cheeseburgers, etc. Then you still got the main line.

Middle school made me feel like a big kid, if that makes sense. That's when you get lockers, and your locker is like your own form of identity and your first piece of property. Also, that's when you are introduced to the scheduled classes. You're in a class, the bell rings, and you've got five minutes to get to your next class. It's another level of responsibility added to your life. For me, that was a huge deal. I had heard about it and seen it because of my older brother, but finally getting to experience that was just a whole new world.

My grandmother worked as a janitor at the school. She's always had a one-track mind: Work, work, work. She's very dependable, very reliable. Always has been that way. If she needed to be somewhere or have us somewhere, she'd leave the house two to three hours early. She won't drive the interstate, period. Never did when I was young and she was in her 50s. Still, to this day, no. Highway and back roads only. She's not getting on an interstate. You can hang it up.

There were benefits of her working at the school. I'd sit in the custodian office and watch TV, or she'd help my lunch be microwaved. You almost feel superior, above the rules. It's like, you know your grandmother is there. The teachers liked her too. I can recall a few times when I would get disciplined a little bit different than what the standard may be for a lot of kids.

Not that I would get away with everything. Some teachers were harder on me because my mouth was getting me in trouble a lot. I never got to go on a field trip as a reward for good behavior. Never, in all three years. If you didn't get too many demerits, they'd take everybody to the zoo. I always had to stay back at the school because I'd always get demerits. My teachers used to write those things up like bills. Chewing gum, talking while the teacher's talking, late to class, getting a hall pass and I'm gone for 20 minutes.... But instead of sending me to the principal, it may be a conversation after class. Or the teachers would inform my grandmother and tell her to handle it instead of saying, "Go see Mrs. Honeyman," the principal that nobody wanted to go visit.

Since I've been alive, my grandma's been a big cigarette smoker. My cousin and I use to hide her cigarettes, hoping that'd get her to quit, but it just pissed her off. She lived down the road from us with Pork Chop. I can remember sitting in his lap while he'd read me stories. He was narcoleptic, so he'd fall asleep in a snap. My granny used to be pissed whenever I would get in the car with him. Any time he'd go somewhere, I'm trying to get in there too. Every time! One time, we had a little fender bender. He rear-ended somebody not too far from the house and she had to come up there and help. Before she even checked to see if we were all right, she's going off about me even being in the car with him.

The acre tract that they were living on was nothing great. He had at minimum eight or nine cars parked out front like a car lot, as if he were trying to sell them. There was an old schoolhouse in the front yard where he sold liquor on Sundays, when the real liquor stores were closed. He was just a business-oriented guy with a lot of different things to earn income. We might be in the house with Granny and he'd have guys pull up, like his friend Richie, an older guy who came around damn near every Sunday. At that age I'm thinking he's just coming by to visit. Now that I'm older, I can see he was coming by to buy a pint.

Pork Chop used to collect coins too. He had treasury safes full of pennies and quarters. Big jars stacked of these things. Probably thousands of dollars' worth of coins, just coins. One time, my brother and I found where he kept his cash. We were being nosy, fumbling around the house, and reached in one of his jacket pockets. He had an envelope that he kept in there. Nothing but hundreds. We got a couple of them hundreds out too. Every so often, we would go check the envelope, see if it had grown, and we might slide a hundred out. At 11 or 12 years old, a hundred dollars is a lot of money. That would hold you over for a little bit. And go about our business. I don't think he knew, or he didn't pay much attention to it. We never got caught doing it.

In December 2006, when I was 12 years old, Pork Chop passed away unexpectedly in the VA Hospital. His death hit harder than I expected, to be honest. That one hurt. My mother's father lived in Detroit but we'd only see him once in a blue moon. My dad's father lived somewhere up north as well. So, Pork Chop was really my only grandfather figure. We rented our home from him, and couple of years after he died, his family decided to auction off all of his properties for financial gain, so we were forced to find a new place to live.

My granny and Porkchop lived shouting distance from our cousins Brion and Brandon and we lived not even two miles down the street. Whenever you saw one of us, normally you'd see all four of us. We spent countless nights together growing up, doing anything and everything. Their home was very small as well, with two bedrooms and one bathroom. But at that age, their situation seemed better than our situation, mainly because their mother (who is my mom's cousin) had her own room, while Brion and Brandon had the other room. At our place, the three of us still shared one room.

Brion spent a lot of time writing music because he wanted to pursue a rap career—and he was good at it. I was 12 at the time but I was getting in at these teen nights at the skating rink in Mt. Juliet. They called it Freestyle Friday and he would perform every Friday night. That was his thing. Never played sports. Music was his industry. For about a month straight, he won every Friday. We were like, "Damn, Brion might have a future in rap." He was winning so often that his mom and some of his family ended up coming to one of the teen nights.

Brandon is my age, the shortest one of the group, light-skinned, and very chubby at the time. We teased him all the time, especially when it was time for hide and seek. He was always, by design, the first person you'd go after, just because he was heavy. When it came to running or anything of that nature, Brandon never could sustain, so we had a lot of jokes about that.

Brion and Brandon were both shorter than my brother and me. If we were outside playing basketball, football, or softball, it was always two-on-two. Brion and Brandon versus my brother and me. Always. It never mixed. The majority our first experiences were with one another. We'd fight each other and come back outside tomorrow like nothing happened. Their mother, Cámara, was very strict and outspoken. We lived so close in proximity together, we could be in our yard playing a game and she could scream from her porch and we could hear it. We kind of feared her because she was so outspoken and because she's the type that will walk in the house and just be like, "Y'all need to take y'all ass outside."

At this point, Dad was in prison and Pork Chop was gone too. But I remember there was one specific male who used to be around. We'll call him Rick.

This was when it was cool to have sound systems in your trunk. Rick had woofers so loud that you would hear him before you saw him. We'd all be outside playing basketball and you could literally hear this man down the street. These speakers used to get our attention all the time. We loved hearing that.

Rick was Brion and Brandon's stepfather, but they called him Dad because their biological father was not around. To me, Rick's lifestyle was very intriguing. Mind you, I already knew about this extravagance with my own father, and it was still present in my life even though my dad wasn't around. That type of glitter was still in my face. Rick would interact with us often and talk trash to us all the time. He was the first guy I knew to iron his money because he wanted it that straight. He was always aesthetically together. Clothes fresh, nice crease, new shoe boxes stacked to the ceiling in the house.

To the world he was a street-oriented man and a member of a gang known as the Crips. To me, he was Brion and Brandon's stepdad who looked out for us. They lived in a very small house that they rented from Pork Chop. We would always be over there, or at my house across the street, or at my granny's house next door, doing something collectively. I remember like yesterday calling their house phone to see if they could come outside and play. Cámara would tell me, "No, they not coming outside today because they didn't clean them dishes!"

That was always the worst news you could hear when one of them was grounded from coming outside. Their mom played zero games growing up, very strict. She worked long hours like my mom, so all of us kids spent a lot of time alone. The only time you'd really catch Rick at home for any amount of time is if he was in there asleep. He was never still for too long. He was always on the move. When he's up, he's getting ready to roll. He'd come back, gone again. I believe Rick used to work on cars, because he kept a job, but he was just always in and out.

If I had to say, watching how their stepdad operated for sure influenced my mind to fast money and street activity. Not because he ever tried to persuade me to want to be in a gang, but it was seeing his lifestyle, understanding how he lived. I had friends my age who were already involved in gangs. I'm like, "OK, if I go get with the people my age, by the time I get to be Rick's age, then I'll be having nice things like him." You see what I'm saying? Basically, "I can do what he's doing, just on a kid scale." That's when I thought, "Man, that's the life. I'm about to start getting some money."

By this time, Brion was already a few steps ahead of Brandon and me with his life experiences. I never knew how he would get it, but I found out that from time to time he may have access to marijuana. When I heard that Brandon had already tried it once, I figured it couldn't be that bad.

I got high for my first time in eighth grade with Brandon, Brion, and two other friends. We hotboxed one of Brion's cars, which means that you sit inside of a vehicle, with all the windows rolled up, and you pass the blunt around. When you're blowing the smoke, it stays in the car. Didn't know what I was doing really, but I know I felt extremely lifted. I'm like, "Dang, so this is what it's like." I knew what weed was because I had friends that were doing it since, hell, sixth grade. I was never brave enough to do it. But suddenly in Brion's old-school bronze Cutlass, I was like a kid in a candy store. Couldn't believe I did it, but at the same time, I was like, "I'm cool now." Their grandma, who was out of town that weekend, lived right next door to them, so we went in her house with the munchies, eating everything in the damn house.

Before I ever started smoking weed, we used to take paper out of the dictionary, roll the paper up as if it was some type of cigar, and smoke the damn paper. We called them "runtz," like a knockoff version of blunts. We weren't even necessarily inhaling. We just wanted the experience of blowing smoke out of our mouth. In between the runtz and the weed, that's when Brandon and I started stealing Granny's cigarettes, or we'd get the cigarette butts that she finished and go light the rest of that. There might be a little bit of tobacco left on it. We'd go sit in one of Pork Chop's abandoned cars outside and just lean back and smoke.

My brother was heavily involved in high school sports, so between sports and his girlfriend, he was rarely around. He'd kick it with us, but he didn't smoke with us. However, I'm the one that introduced my brother to marijuana. I was like, "Man, you got to try this. It's gonna have you feeling crazy." Then I'd invite some other friends over and we might hit a blunt or two in the cars outside. Now, with the friends, we didn't smoke regularly. I think it was something they wanted to do, but it was one of those things—now that they know Dee had done it, they're going to try it. I ended up becoming that bad influence, because among my friends who hadn't yet been introduced, now I'm taking it to them. As an adult I have thought about that, because it could have ignited a vice that was already within them. Life has taken a couple of them down a severe weed-smoking path and some legal trouble as well. I wonder, in their mind, if they think I'm the one that activated something that was already in them.

At this point, I'm hanging out with some young guys outside of school who are involved in gang activity. I can't remember exactly what the situation was, but some of those friends ran the same area that Brion and Brandon's stepfather ran. My friends claimed to be Bloods and Rick was claimed to be a

Crip. One day, my gang friends had some words with Brion over MySpace, I think. I don't know exactly what it was, but it ended up getting back to Rick. These Bloods were threatening to fight him, and Brion told Rick that I had been running with these young dudes.

Before I could do anything about it, Rick came up on me as if I was a grown man, yelling, "Where them dudes at? Go ahead, get them on the phone. Get them on the phone! We can do this right now!" Mind you, I'm a young teenager, 13 years old, and this is a man in his 30s. He attempted to pressure me, as if I was another gang member. To this day, that could have been by design, just showing me this shit is for real out here. You don't need to be running around here playing. But there was never a conversation about it after that.

I got spooked, like, "Damn, I ain't got nothing to do with gangs." Which, in reality, I didn't. But to my peers and friends, it seemed as if I was involved. However, it really didn't have anything to do with me. I was one step from it, though. Easily. After that, I stayed out of it. I ain't built for this. This ain't what I like. I was damn near looking out the window every night, making sure Rick wasn't coming back for me.

Starting my eighth-grade year, Brandon and I got suspended from the school bus a couple of times for silly things. Throwing stuff out of the window, maybe standing up while the bus driver was driving. Making her job extremely hard. Then, just a few weeks into the school year, we went too far. When you're kicked off the bus for the remainder of the year, you got to be doing something crazy.

I can recall specifically that it happened at the transfer spot, where the middle school bus and the high school bus would meet. While the buses were parked, Brandon and I made a deal with each other, like, "Hey, let's walk down the aisle and intentionally fall into somebody's seat and see what they do." Brandon's leading the charge, walking down the aisle, falling into people's seats, and looking for a reaction. After a few rows of that, he falls onto this one guy. I don't know if this guy's having a bad day or what, but he pushes Brandon away. I saw that and I was like, "He ain't going to do me like that."

So, I follow behind Brandon and fell into this same guy's seat and he pushes me out of the seat too. It doesn't turn into a fight, but it turns into a small scuffle. I'm pushing him around and really antagonizing him.

Right at that moment, the high schoolers were transferring onto the bus, so here comes my brother and Brion. I wasn't able to get the ups on this young individual and the situation ended quicker than I wanted it to. As I'm walking back to my seat, I slapped the guy. This kid is literally minding his own business and I slapped him.

The following morning in the principal's office, I was shown the entire film. Right above the bus driver, there's a camera facing all the seats and anyone could see the whole situation. The footage was clear as day. There wasn't really any explaining necessary. Brandon and I tried our best to come up with a great lie to tell our moms, because they didn't see the film. I think we dressed it up to where we were defending ourselves, but it didn't hold any weight because regardless of what we're saying, we can't ride the bus anymore. However, because my grandmother worked at the school, I still had a ride.

Around this same time, I got into my first fistfight. I was a loose cannon, a rebel, the prime definition. And it was over something very minor. We were out ding-dong ditching, where you knock on somebody's door or ring their doorbell, then run and hide somewhere to watch them come to the door. We noticed two friends in the neighborhood who were riding their bikes. We tried to recruit them to come with us. One of the kids says, "No, I'm riding bikes with my friend." So, I'm like, "Damn, man, stop acting like a ho." Then he made the comment, "Your mom was a ho when I put my ... in her last night." This is what he says. Then he rides off on his bike.

My pride kicks in and my friends say to me, "Are you going to let him talk to you like that?" I said, "When I see him, I got him." As we continued ding-dong ditching, my friends are really gassing the situation, saying, "I know you're not going to let him get away with that." I'm like, "When I see him, I'm going to whoop his ass." And they're like, "You ain't going to do nothing."

We end up circling the block, looking for him. The neighborhood wasn't huge, but at the time it felt huge. By this time, we see them. They've put their bikes up, so they're on foot. We're coming down the street and they're coming from the left. My friends say, "There they go, right there."

Now it's like an adrenaline rush. I'd told my friends what I was going to do and they think I ain't going to do it. When I cornered that kid, I was like, "What exactly was that you said about my mama now?" He was like, "What do you mean? I didn't say nothing." At this point I'm up on him: "Repeat that!" Face to face: "Repeat that!" Before he could even say a word, I just grab him, tackle him to the ground, and start hitting him. I'm straddled on top of him, talking to him at the same time, "Don't you ever..."

After that my friends were kind of like, "Damn, you really did that." But that was the end of it. It ain't like I sent him to the hospital. It wasn't nothing vicious. To my friends it was like ... I don't know, just a sense of accomplishment, I guess. They were praising it like, "You just whooped his ass." Here we are, 13 years old.

Just to add to my rebelliousness, I decided not to play basketball that year. We got a new basketball coach who quickly got word on my disruptive behavior during school. He told me and a few other kids, "I'd love to have you on this team, but I don't need you. I'm not putting up with your behavior. If I get one report of demerits, you guys are kicked off the team."

Me being me, I don't mess with that and I'm not playing. "Who you talking to, bro? My granny works here. I do what I want." At this point, I was still playing AAU basketball, so my ego was really growing. I'm slightly involved in the streets, I smoke weed, I'm feeling untouchable. Now, all of a sudden, you're hearing, "Dee ain't playing basketball? What? What's really going on?" The coach didn't budge. He didn't beg for me to play. Nothing.

I did play football that year, though, but I didn't get on the field much because I had broken my arm. Again. The first time I broke it, I was in fourth grade, and I tried to tell my mom. She didn't take me to the hospital for a week! She told me, "Take some ibuprofen, put some ice on it, and go to sleep." And every day I'm waking up with pain. On the playground a few days later, I was trying to push myself up and it shifted again. I said, "I've got to go to the hospital." Finally she took me, and sure enough, broken.

Now, fresh out of a cast for the second time, I didn't know what to do with myself. Without playing on the school team, I figured I would play rec league and try out again in high school. At that age, college was nowhere in sight. I didn't think about playing college ball. I didn't think about basketball being able to change my life. I had no knowledge of that. But to just say I'm not playing, that was odd.

That was a moment of vulnerability, admitting to myself, "Maybe I do need to be on this team." Because somebody has stepped into your life and said they're going to implement structure and discipline, you're basically saying, "Hell no"? It was an ego check. I had to get off the pedestal that I really didn't have. My imaginary pedestal that I thought I was on, I had to get off that and snap out of it. Snap into reality and just understand that, man, if you want something you going to have to fight for it. Ain't nobody going to give you nothing. I had to seek it out and open my mouth to receive that. I had to put my pride to the side.

It was hard for me to do. My mom told me, "Oh, just go in there and talk to him." Some of my friends were saying, "I think he'll let you come back on team." Nobody forced me to do it. I can still see myself slowly walking into the locker room, and as I look back on it as an adult, that was a perfect time to experience that firsthand, humbling myself to get something that in reality I really wanted. A kid coming in there with that type of initiative probably caught him off guard.

I wanted to play. When we spoke, I told him, "I want to give it another try. I do want to try to play on the team. I think I can act right." At this point, they were already two or three weeks into practice. He said, "I'm going to meet with the team and take a vote. It's going to be their decision. If you get enough votes, and they're OK with you coming back after missing all the conditioning in the preseason, then we'll allow it to happen. I'll meet with you tomorrow."

One guy did say no. He was a sixth grader at the time and said he didn't know who I was. He thought it was going to affect his playing time. But the rest of the team said yeah, so I ended up getting on the team that year and we had a heck of a year. Even though we didn't win it, we made it to state tournament.

The lesson I got from it is, no matter who you think you may be, there are in times in life when you need to humble yourself. You're not above or superior to anyone or anything. If you want something, go after it. You can't allow your pride or the fear of rejection stop you from trying to reach something you're trying to obtain.

After middle school basketball ended, we'd go up to the high school for workouts to get ready for the football season in August. That summer, my friend Austin liked to take his mom's Grand Am out for a joy ride with some of his other friends. He never bothered to ask permission and he always got away with it. None of us even had a license yet. Finally, feeling left out, I built up enough courage to join them. Of course, Brandon came too. There were four of us, all incoming freshman on the football team. Inside the vehicle, we drank a few Smirnoffs and smoked some Black & Milds. That was it. We didn't go extremely far, probably five to ten miles away, to some young ladies' houses whose parents weren't home.

When Austin's mom woke up the following morning, she noticed mud on the tires. Ashes from the Black & Milds were all over the front seat. And we left a Smirnoff bottle in the backseat. Obviously it aroused questions. I don't know how that situation went with him and her, but she called my mom to explain the situation, and my mom just went ballistic. I'll never forget that. She told me I'm grounded for the remainder of the year. There wasn't any physical punishment, but she threatened me verbally and took my phone. I could not go anywhere outside of school. Any recreation, hanging out with friends—that's over with. No video games, which for me, that's huge. After I stole that car, I didn't go nowhere.

My mom used to always say, "You don't apply yourself." Or "If you knew your homework like you know them damn songs, you'd be all right." To be honest, I didn't give a flying hell about school. Did not. I've always been intelligent, but I never did apply myself. But it ain't like I had scholars in my family. Nobody had graduated college except my dad, and I didn't grow up with him. I came from a family of high school diplomas. So, to be so intentional and focused on school, that wasn't heard of.

Those middle school years were a very big transition for me. I was dealing with a lot, having an identity crisis, out here doing lord knows what. My mom was sending letters to my dad in prison about how I was behaving, so he was guilt-tripping and fearing that his son was fixing to go down that same path, but even with those internal battles, there was nothing he could do about it.

While I'm going through all of this in middle school, I couldn't see how big the elephant is, because I'm right up on it. But now that I look at it, I'm like, damn boy your middle school was kind of treacherous. All of my influence was just dead ends, negative, pessimistic. None of it had any rhyme or reason or any type of brightness to it. My influence back then was either money or instant gratification. What I would tell my younger self, or somebody in those shoes now, is to surround yourself with positive influence. At that time, I didn't have any.

4
THIN ICE

Doing all these crazy things in middle school, and later in high school, I never considered my future. I didn't even think that far ahead. That's the lesson of not having any type of sense of direction or positive influence or representation about you. You only think for right now. You think in the moment. Before you know it, you've made a decision that could cost you, whether it's financial or whether it's some of your time. When you don't have any positive representation or any type of positive influence, you don't even fathom thinking beyond what's going to happen for the next hour. I mean, you're really in "survival of the fittest" mode, just doing stuff that makes sense right then. I had no rhyme or reason to be doing what I was doing.

There was no possible pleasure that I could get out of smoking in the bathroom in my freshman year. Now that I look back at it, being in that rebellious stage, I just didn't care. In the fall of my freshman year at Wilson Central, my friends went into the bathroom during school hours to smoke. There was a trend going around school at that time, along the lines of exhaling into a light bulb, which basically vaporized the smoke and kept the fumes from getting out into the hallway. At that age, everything is a temptation and an adrenaline rush, just wondering, "Can I get away with it?" So, my friends are saying, "Dude, we were upstairs by such-and-such's classroom during second period, smoking in the bathroom. Nobody knew."

This was on game day, during basketball season, late November or early December. One of those friends told me, "We're going to come by your classroom today and do it again." Each classroom door has a slit window and later that day I saw my friends out in the hall, like, "Come on out!" I was in English class and asked to go to the bathroom. When we were in the bathroom, doing our thing, I was so paranoid. I knew I didn't need to be doing this. I think I hit a Black & Mild one time, if that. My friends were like, "Man, I'm going stand in here to finish this," and I ended up getting out of there, going back to class.

It wasn't 20 minutes after, here comes the principal and the campus police knocking on my classroom door. "Can we see Mr. Darrius Oldham?" In my mind, I'm thinking, "There's no way they know about that. Not that fast." They escorted me to the assistant principal's office. When I walked in, my two friends were already sitting in there with their backpacks. Once I saw that, I knew. The principal and assistant principal said they could smell the smoke in the hall, and they watched the cameras and saw us coming out of there.

The principal said, "Can you get your backpack?" So, I did, and they searched everything we had. We had to empty our pockets. I didn't have anything on me. I told them, "I have no idea what you're talking about." There was no proof that I had smoked. I told them that I just happened to be in the bathroom at the wrong time. I was like, "I don't know anything about that."

None of us admitted to smoking. However, when they found the tobacco on my friend, he got expelled and sent to alternative school. I don't remember him shaking back from that. I think he came back to school the following year, but it was still rocky. It just was never the same for him.

The school called my mom about it, but there was no proof to suspend me. I told her the same lie, that I just happened to be in the wrong place at the wrong time. So, she's giving me the spiel about, "You need to watch who you're around. You ain't got no business being around that stuff anyway. Why wasn't your ass in class?"

That's what you call playing with fire. Had they walked in the bathroom while we were there, I would have been busted in the act. I think I ended up getting in-school suspension, just for being gone from class too long. Nothing severe. I know I played the game that night. But the reality of it is, I just didn't get caught. I smoked just like the kid who went to alternative school. The difference between getting caught and not getting caught doesn't change the fact that you did it.

As another example, Brandon and I would skip first and second block all the time. I would already be at the school for basketball practice in the morning, but Brandon rode the bus in because he didn't play sports. I would let him in the side door by the locker room, and then we would sneak out and go down the highway to Waffle House until about 10 o'clock. Afterwards, we'd check in at school. As long as you were there for two periods, it was considered a full day. One time, Brandon and one of our friends got caught skipping and got suspended. The campus officers watched them on camera leaving in their vehicle. Most mornings, I was in the locker room, which is already in a secluded area. I would always enter and exit the building by the boys' locker room, so I left in a different direction. Lo and behold, they didn't catch me.

I played quarterback in my freshman year but our football team was terrible. Going into basketball season, I was still kind of chubby and out of shape. Nothing too exceptional. Our head coach, Coach Love, used to be hard on me. He's another guy that always says he could see the talent, but I obviously didn't know what I had. He was the only black coach I had up until college. He could relate to my home life and my situation. He showed us you've got to have some tough skin to survive. You've got to be tough. He's a walking inspiration.

The summer between my freshman and sophomore year, I didn't get much playing time on my AAU team. It became "daddy ball," because I played for a coach whose son was on the team. I was one of only two black kids on the team. Nobody mistreated me but they never gave me really a fair chance. So that killed a lot of my confidence.

In the preseason leading into my sophomore basketball year, I started to make a little bit of a jump. I was still inconsistent though, because I didn't truly believe I was good. I couldn't string four quarters together. I might come out the first half and score 14, then end the game with 15 points. Or have two points in the first half but go crazy in the second half and end the game with 18. I never could put four quarters together as a sophomore. I wasn't extremely athletic, coming through dunking on people. I wasn't extremely fast, so I had to be a little more versatile. Also, I didn't shoot any three pointers. All my points were two points. One of my high school coaches would tell me, "The difference between you going to a Division I college and a community college is going to be you learning how to shoot this three. That's going to be the difference."

We weren't a very good team in my sophomore year. We would go play other schools before the season started and I remember I finally had a breakout scrimmage, like everybody wondering, "Damn, where did this come from?" I was playing extremely well and it sparked some momentum. I mean, I had a day! I was scoring at a high rate. The goal felt like an ocean. I couldn't miss. My adrenaline was going. Coach was like, "What's gotten into you?" He was looking for that one guy to step up and be the man.

These weren't overly packed games because they didn't really count for anything. Scrimmages are just a way to get an early look at teams, but there were definitely people in the stands. Because I lacked confidence on the court, my confidence came from seeing the ball go through the net. If I'm missing shots, I'm beating myself up and not understanding there's way more to the game than just scoring. Just feeling sorry for myself. But if I'm making shots, oh yeah! I'm playing defense and I'm ready to go.

My sophomore year is when it started to click. Suddenly I had something to build momentum off of. People were looking forward to my next two years. At this point, my brother is playing football as a freshman at UT Chattanooga. That motivated me. Now the conversation's starting to circulate a little bit, like, "Well, you still got two more years of high school basketball. If you polish this and work on this, you got a chance to play college ball." I started to take my craft a little more seriously. Then I found out I needed an 18 on my ACT test for any college to even consider me.

My GPA was always OK, like 3.1. My mom would tell me, "We need to test and just measure, and see where you are." That way, I would have two years to see if I needed new ACT preps. When I took the ACT for my first time in the 10th grade, I fell asleep during the test. Made a 14. I think you get a 13 for just putting your name on it. I'm being serious! I think you get a 13 for just filling it out. That shows you my lack of focus at that time.

During my freshman and sophomore years in school, I'm not really giving a damn. I'm doing enough to where I'm not failing, so that I'm staying eligible. But I'm not caring, for real. I'm not doing any extra studying. I'm cramming for a test. If I know I got a test, the period before I'm looking over the notes, trying to just memorize it real quick. Or I'm that kid that's right here looking over your shoulder, cutting eyes.

Directly after my sophomore year, an elite club called The MidState Ballerz reached out to me on Facebook, to tell me about their tryouts. They played on a bigger circuit and I knew they had produced quite a few college athletes. Some very, very nice college players had played for that program previously. A lot of college coaches came to their showcases, so that felt like my chance to really get on the scene.

At this time, my high school basketball coach convinced me to quit football altogether. He said, "You don't love that sport. You don't care to have a future in football. And you're risking severe injuries and not being able play basketball." A selfish thing for him to do, but I understand why he did that. He wanted me for his team.

So, junior year comes and our basketball team was projected to have a damn good team that year. We were young. We only had two seniors, so almost everybody would be back again next year. I'm playing well, averaging about 16 or 17 points a game as a junior. I'm starting to get my swagger right. As time is going on, I'm steadily getting better. I'm finding my momentum. I'm maturing more. The trouble in school is dwindling down at this point. I might get into trouble for having my phone out or something, but the rebellious antics are gone. When I paid for another ACT test and stayed awake for it, I got a 16. However, our school also offered a free ACT test to every junior, so I took that one and scored a 17.

I'm starting to form my own identity at this point, transforming into a young adult. At semifinals a week earlier, I came out with 32 points against Hendersonville and I'm on fire. Then I had 20 points and a home court advantage when we beat Lebanon High School to reach the top four. At that game, I got elbowed in the jaw, so I'd been in the hospital all night with a busted mouth full of stitches. With maybe four hours of sleep the night before, I remember telling my teammate and best friend, Tyler, that I was running on fumes and adrenaline.

That Saturday night, we're about to play our biggest game of the year against Gallatin High on their court. The winner goes on to the district championship game, but the loser has to play for either third or fourth in the district. We played Gallatin in the regular season. I think we beat them once and they beat us once. They were a good team, but only one of us would advance to the championship game.

Our fans are in the stadium. Gallatin's fans are still in the stadium. The fans of both teams that played before us are still in the stadium. The women's tournament is held there too, so those teams were in the stadium. It's loud and it's packed. Man, it's everybody in there, for real.

I scored about 30 points that game, but all night the score's going back and forth. With 4.3 seconds left in the game, we're down one point and trying to score. Unbelievably we end up turning the ball over and Gallatin steals it, so we fouled to freeze the game. Their guy shoots two free throws and makes both. Now we're down three points and we've got to go the length of the court. My teammate inbounds me the ball and I catch it. I take about two dribbles, get it across half court, and heave it. Horn goes off.

Nailed it.

The shot goes in. A three-pointer. Sends us into overtime but you really would have thought we just won the game. I ran all the way across the court, directly to the Gallatin student section, talking trash, yelling, "Y'all can't touch me!" But it's loud so nobody can hear what I'm saying. It's all showboating because they were giving me a hard time all game. Doing what fans do, just trying to get in your head.

First overtime, still tied. Second overtime, same thing. The game ends up going to triple overtime. I can't remember if the game was tied or if we were up by one, but whatever the situation was, a guy on the Gallatin team gets the ball inbounds and we trap him immediately. He steps through the trap, splits it. The horn goes off and he shoots the ball anyway. And the damn ball goes in the goal. But there was no signal from the referees and the shot was clearly after the horn. Then the referees run off the court. Normally, a referee would either signal if it's good or no good, but they just sprint off the court.

Immediately the Gallatin student section storms the court, going crazy, picking up the players. Meanwhile, the referees disappear out the gym door to get to their locker room and out of the chaos. They get out of there quick. Then I see our assistant coach sprinting after them, like "What's the call? What's going on?" When I see that, the old Oldham kicks in. Trouble time. I'm fishing for it. I light up. Let's see what I can do and get away with.

I see my coach run and I take off running too. I'm weaving through the crowd, not paying attention to the fact that they're celebrating. I ain't worried about none of that. By the time the refs had cleared the door where Coach was headed, the police had blocked it. I see that ahead of me, so I cut through the side door and come up a side hallway. Nobody's over there and I start looking around. I can hear the people flooding into the lobby but I'm looking for the refs. Then I see them back in this cut in the hallway, so I swiftly turn the corner and we're face to face. It's almost like a stare-off. I'm looking at them, they're looking at me. Ain't no words in exchange. So, I'm like, "Oh, that's what we doing?"

Again, this goes back to what I talked about sophomore year. I'm thinking only in the moment. I'm not even knowing what I'm going to do. My adrenaline's running, I'm still sweating. I turn around and see the double doors with an exit sign right there above them. I reach up and I punch that sign as hard as I can. Wham! It shatters everywhere. An off-duty cop I hadn't noticed in the hallway saw me do it. As soon as I hit that sign, he grabbed me. He wasn't in uniform. I still remember he had on a sweater and some khakis. He's a big ol' officer too. Probably about 6'7. Big boy.

At first, I'm like, "Who is this grabbing me? Get off me!" Then he shouts, "You're under arrest for destruction of school property and vandalism." He doesn't have handcuffs with him, so he's holding my arms and escorts me into the middle of the crowd. By this time, the same officers that had hemmed up Coach at that door have made it out into the lobby area. When one of those officers sees me, he rushes over like I have killed somebody and slaps the cuffs on.

This is just two or three weeks after my brother's accident and of course it's still playing on my mind. But this time, the cuffs are on me. I'm still in my basketball uniform, sweating, and kind of in shock. I can hear people screaming for my mom, like, "Kim! They got Dee!" Then here she comes, flying off the bleachers, like, "Get the hell out of my way!" The officers are backing me out of the gym and everybody's looking at me, like, "Whoa! What's wrong?" Everybody thought I hit a ref. Even the newspaper article the next day said something like, "Wilson Central Star Player Arrested for Punching Referee."

By the time the officers get me out in the hallway, my mom bumps hard through the door, like "What's going on? The only reason you all got them cuffs on him is because he black." She went to that point immediately. She kept asking, "What'd he do?" They wouldn't tell her. They said, "Ma'am, we're not answering any questions. You can come downtown to booking and figure out everything you need to know." That's when she started pulling the race card, saying, "No, y'all ain't taking him nowhere." Now my granny's coming and she's popping off. My granddaddy from Detroit, who'd just retired and moved back to LaGuardo, kept saying to my mom, "He's going to be all right." He was so even-keeled all the time, but she's like, "No! Hell no!"

At this point, they sat me down so I'm sitting crisscross applesauce in handcuffs on the floor. Everybody's still coming out of the game and filing past, asking me, "You good? Are you good?" If I ain't, what y'all going to do? I don't want to talk to nobody, so I'm just sitting there shaking my head. At this point, I'm crying, really. Not like boohoo, but tears are flowing out of my eyes. I'm still mad about the game. I'm scared because I'm thinking they really are about to detain me. I'm confused, don't know what's going on. I'm like, "Damn, what the fuck have I done?"

My mama's steady going off until the principal gets her to the side. Then the cops slowly lead me through the crowd, like a walk of shame. Down the hallway in a back room somewhere, they take the cuffs off me. I don't know how the conversation went, but they end up not taking me to juvenile. Somehow I wind up in the locker room and Coach tells the whole team, "Everybody get on the bus. Ain't nobody taking a ride." Normally after a game, you can ride home with your parents if you didn't need to go back to the school. But he said, "We're getting out here as a team. Tell your parents to pick you up at the school." He told us, "People are going to be texting you, but we ain't answering no questions."

Back at the school, I rolled with one of my friends back toward home, because he lived over there. My mom had calmed down at that point, but she still was upset. She wasn't angry with me, but I can only imagine as a mother, within the span of a month, dealing with both of your kids damn near fighting charges. "You don't know how much it crushed my heart to see both of my kids in handcuffs three weeks apart," she confided in me later. "I just dealt with this with your brother, and here you are, cuffed up as well."

I can see how that makes a mother feel like she has no control. And I think she did have a point playing the race card, for sure. Granted, I did punch the sign. I did destruct some property. But I think they went overboard. I think they very well went overboard. Sumner County is known for things like that. Black people have a hard time over there and not just the juveniles. When black people get in trouble, they have a hard time in those court systems. They always say you do not want to go to jail in Sumner County. They make it hard on you.

I ended up suspended for one game, which we lost to Clarksville Northeast. That's how our season ended. The coach wasn't really tripping on the suspension because we were bringing almost everybody back, except a couple of seniors. We had plans to go to state the next year. He was basically saying, "We're going to get over this hump, put it behind us and move forward."

It was a hell of a lesson. I can honestly say I don't have any regrets. Man, I don't regret anything I have ever done because I learned so much from it. I'm definitely thankful that things didn't go the other routes that they could have, but I don't have any regrets, man. I'm blessed.

From that, most importantly I learned emotional intelligence, meaning that it's vital to control your emotions. You can trick yourself out of your position by acting irate. Whether that's somebody saying something to you that you may not necessarily like, or just a situation happening that upsets you.

Before you know it, you might go ballistic, and you can miss a lot of opportunities with that. Depending on your place of employment, you can get fired. You can ruin some friendships, if you talk crazy to somebody you don't agree with. Regardless how a situation makes you feel handle it with professionalism. There's nothing wrong with feeling these emotions and being upset, but you have to be careful how you portray that.

My high school coach used to always say, "You need to be like a surfer." Don't ever get too high, and don't ever get too low. When you get overly anxious, excited, or arrogant, you are going to fall off the wave. If you get too low, if you too depressed, too sad, too low on the wave, you are going to drown, or the wave is going to hit you. Stay right in the middle and ride the wave. Ride that wave like a surfer and you are going to ride that wave forever.

5

BETTER MAN

When my season ended with that Gallatin game, I still had a lot left in the tank to show, and I felt like we could have made it to state that year. I'm finally starting to get momentum, and then boom, I get suspended, it's stripped away from me, and I literally watched my team compete without me from the bench in a suit and tie. I could see my impact more than ever then because it looked like a completely different scene without me on the floor.

My coach agreed to that suspension, instead of trying to appeal it, because all the core guys on our team were returning the following year. We didn't want any kind of misconception or issues with TSSAA, which is the organization that runs high school sports in Tennessee. Going into the next year, we didn't want them to say, "OK, he's suspended for the beginning of the first six games of next year," or whatever. We conformed to what they presented and said, "Let's get this over with," because next year would likely be a big year.

After that experience against Gallatin, I was hungrier than ever. I knew that every game counted, as far as trying to get exposure. That suspension felt like an unsatisfied ending, like a relationship with no closure where you just get left on the cliff. I played one more AAU season with the MidState Ballerz on the 17-and-under team, but I was having a mediocre summer. I'm still playing for the same coach that I played for the previous year. It's roughly the same team and I'm still not really separating myself. Still getting no college recognition.

I'd become friends with a personal trainer named Dre Garner by this time. Dre was a family friend of my childhood friend, Austin, who happened to play for our crosstown rivals. Dre and Austin's family also attended church together. Dre would come watch local tournaments, check in with me here and there, but I still was giving him the runaround. He hadn't gotten his hands on me yet. He would tell me, "If you start working with me, I'm going to have you the best in the city." This is how he's talking. Mind you, he didn't even play college basketball. His football career ended in high school after a severe car wreck. So, I'm looking at him like, "How are you going to get me to do something that you've never done?" In my mind, I still had that attitude.

In AAU, July is called the "live period," which means that college coaches can watch the teams every day that month. One of our guys who was getting recruited could dunk on anybody, and some of my other teammates were getting college looks as well. I felt like I was just as good as them and I couldn't understand why I wasn't getting any offers. At the time, I wasn't as athletic as those guys, so maybe that was part of the reason, but I'm thinking, "I can still do X, Y and Z." The disconnect was, I didn't consistently believe that I could perform at that level.

When we were showcasing in Florida, our AAU assistant coach was evaluating our college prospects on the team, telling us what he thought our ceiling was. He told a couple other guys that he thought they could be Division I players. That's the top level we're all striving for. Then he told a couple of others that they had potential to play Division II. I'm just listening. Then he looked at me and said, "I think you can get a chance to play Division III basketball or NAIA."

Division III can't even offer scholarships...

When I bring this up to him now, he says he knew that statement would motivate me, and that's why he said it. But at that time, that's not how he explained it. Imagine him telling me that, and we still had more games to play. I'm already having internal conflicts and he's pouring lemon juice in an open wound. By him telling me that, it ignited something in me to say, "I'm going to do the opposite." That rebellious Dee who always enjoyed going against the grain was back on the scene. The worst thing you can do for me is say I can't do something, because it's going to get done. Now I'm going out on the court with the mindset of, "I'm going to show him wrong." The key components that were used in a negative way as a child were the same reason I begin to excel. I became rebellious to any statement or label one would try to place on me.

August rolls around and I'm in desperation mode. I had been out kicking it with some friends at a shopping center in Mt. Juliet on a Friday night. Afterwards, I was sitting in my car in the movie theater parking lot, and something about that night… it just wasn't satisfying. Hanging out late at night, chasing behind women, was not fulfilling to me. I started doing that at 12 years old, going to teen clubs, so that desire wore down fast. At 17 years old, that wasn't impressive anymore. My senior year's ahead of me but I'm believing that it's unheard of to make a drastic change athletically in a year. So, I'm sitting there alone and telling myself, "I'm going to go all in. If it don't work, it don't work. But it won't be because I didn't try."

I grabbed my phone and texted Dre: "Man, it ain't nothing out here in these streets." Pretty much telling him that I'm willing to do whatever it takes. I'm willing to put the work in to get my game where it needs to go. He responded, "Is everything OK?" Because this message came out of the blue. I was like, "Yeah. I'm good, just let me know what day we start." He asked again, "Are you sure everything is all right, bro?" And I wrote back, "Yeah, I'm good."

Dre was already training a couple of guys in Nashville that played at Belmont University. He told me to meet him the next morning to ride to Belmont with him. Sure enough, I do it. He's working out these guys and he puts me through a core circuit too. Now that I look back at it and my body is trained to do it, it wasn't as tough as I thought it was, but it was for sure an intense core circuit. That day his workout nearly killed me. It wasn't nothing extreme. Strictly resistance bands. It was a different type of work than my body was used to.

He started telling me things like, "If you stick to the script, I'm going to have you the realest individual in the city. Just stick to what I'm telling you, just stick to the script." Or he'd say, "You're going to go through processes to where the body's transforming, and you're going to be feeling sluggish. Just stick to the script." When we started talking about what he charged, I had to tell him, "Man, I can't." He was only asking for maybe a hundred bucks a week, which was $20 to $25 dollars a session, nothing crazy. But I didn't have it. And my mama was like, "No."

We didn't have the money anyway, and even if we did, in her mind it would be like giving it away. She told him to his face, "You can work with him, but I ain't paying you nothing." But to him it wasn't even about the money. He was just trying to help me get into college.

In order to keep working out with Dre, I took a job at Taco Bell. I needed extra cash anyway, partly to pay for the next ACT test coming up, for gas money, and just to have money to hang out with my friends. I knew that when the season started I'd quit Taco Bell, but in the meantime, I needed to get a check. I got paid $180 every two weeks, and because I didn't have any bills and gas was cheap back then, that was sustainable for me. After basketball practice, I'd go work at Taco Bell from 6 p.m. to 10 p.m. Then I'd wake up at 4:30 the next morning to meet Dre.

By this time, I finally had my own car, and boy was I ashamed of that thing. I mean, appearances shouldn't matter really. But again, my internal views played out in everything and that car exposed my reality as a guy who has nothing. I remember that field parties were huge at my high school, and if it was my turn to drive, I would park at a distance and we'd walk up. I wasn't going to pull my car up there.

Mom spotted it for sale on the side of the road. You know how people will write with a big white marker on the front windshield the amount that it costs? "FOR SALE $1600." She was like, "Let me go check that out." It was a two-door 1997 Nissan Sentra, a 200SX. Turquoise green. I was fascinated because it had a sunroof and a CD player, but comparison is the thief of joy. My friends had Nissan Altimas, Pontiacs, Dodge Trucks, Toyotas, etc. And they were up to the model year. Here I am, pulling up in a car where you can hear the brakes before you see me. If I started going over 60 or 70 miles an hour in that car, it would shake. Seriously, it would shake! My friends used to say, "Damn, you the only one that got a car that give us a massage."

With money to pay Dre, we put a regiment together and started out working out at Belmont, local parks, the YMCA, really anywhere. We eventually set up a consistent routine to where we'd meet before school at the YMCA in Donelson, a suburb of Nashville. We worked out Monday and Tuesday mornings, let my body rest on Wednesday, then back in the gym on Thursday and Friday mornings. We'd start at 5 and finish up at about 6:30. Then I would drive about 20 minutes down Central Pike to get to school. I'd have weights from 7:15 to 7:45 at Wilson Central, then school would start at 8:15. So I'd have time to get in there and get a quick shower, get some breakfast, and get ready for class.

Dre was adamant about making my core strong because he believed that everything starts with the core, which is true. Your balance, your ability to run, jump…. A strong core enhances all that. We did core workouts and treadmill sprints every workout. We didn't touch many free weights, like dumbbells, because he believed they impacted your joints. Bad form on weights can really hurt you more than it can help you. Instead, we did a lot of muscle endurance.

We did core work with resistance bands every morning to start our workouts. Depending on the color of the resistance bands, some were harder to pull than others. On our ab circuit, I would lie flat on my back to do crunches, with the resistance band over my head holding me back. It would be 25 crunches straight up, then I'd twist and hold the resistance band to one side for 25 more, working on my obliques. Then twist to the other side, coming up another 25 times. The last set of 25 would be sitting up, rotating to the right, rotating to the left, and coming back down. One hundred crunches, with resistance bands. Brutal.

Dre would always say, "This exercise is going to be the difference." I'd be dripping sweat but I could see my physical transformation, toning up. I mean, I wasn't a bulky guy. I was really frail at this time, and you could see the muscle starting to define. We touched every muscle. On Monday and Thursday, we did upper body, like biceps and triceps, with resistance bands. On Tuesday and Friday, we did lower body, working the hamstrings, quads, hips, calves, and ankles.

Outside of the core, the other thing he emphasized heavily was my cardio condition. You can't get tired. The way good players separate from other players is in that fourth quarter. Anybody can come out with a phenomenal first quarter. Everybody's fresh. Anybody can have a good second quarter, but as the game goes on, when people are wearing down, you still need to be playing at that same first quarter speed.

We followed the Floyd Mayweather workout, where we inclined the treadmill so that it was basically facing the sky, with the incline maxed all the way out. Dre put the speed on 10, so it's flying. I would straddle the treadmill with my feet on the side panels, then I'd jump on while it's moving, and run at a full sprint for 10 seconds on, 20 seconds off. I would do 10 of those. This is how we would end workouts. Every day was core, though. Resistance bands, followed by skill work (usually going into the gym to get up shots or do ball drills around the cones), and ending with cardio. And this was before I went to school, where the team worked out twice a week, with the two other days as open gym.

My mom wasn't the only one against my training at the YMCA. Coach Bond, my high school coach, didn't like it either. I don't want to call him a control freak, but he wanted to be the head man in charge, steering the ship, which is why I felt like he didn't want me playing football. He wanted to have his hands on the entire development of his guys. When he found out I had a trainer, he believed it was going to interrupt what we were doing at school. He considered it going against the grain, trying to do my own thing, becoming an "I guy," listening to the trainer instead of him.

The reason I know that is because he brought it up one time in a timeout. He felt like the team wasn't doing what he said to do. We weren't listening to him, and he shouted: "You're listening to everybody except for me! You got these damn trainers you're working with, and you think they know what's best for you!" He was adamant about that. Coach didn't even like AAU. He felt like it was a cancer because it wasn't structured basketball.

But the thing about it was, he started to see me transform as a player. When the season started later that fall, Dre and I had scaled down our workouts to twice a week. In early November, our team had a scrimmage against Macon County. We were in layup lines, and this is when I knew my work was paying off. I'm skying above the rim at this point, dunking the ball with ease. I could feel the adrenaline. My teammates were looking at me like, "Hold on!

Where the hell did this come from?" Before, I would always run and jump at the rim and try to dunk, but it would be very inconsistent. I might get one out of 10. At this point, I'm dunking with two hands, or maybe even one hand. They're seeing the change too.

By now, I'm starting to get addicted to the process. I'm seeing results. It's a lot easier to start believing what Dre is saying because the results are happening. I'm sticking to the script. What made me trust him? To this day, I still don't have a philosophical answer. However, my back was against the wall. I knew that I had nothing to lose!

My mom still wasn't too fond of the workouts, though, because she didn't like me getting up and leaving the house at 4:30 a.m. Her mind is channeled to think of the worst-case scenario first and she always thinks about what could go wrong versus what can go right. Typical parenting, huh? Sure enough, I was heading to the YMCA one morning and I wasn't even 10 minutes away from my house when a deer ran out in front of me. There was nothing I could do. It happened that quick. BOOM!!! Right after I collided with the deer, it got up and ran off. Meanwhile, my engine is smoking and the front of my hood is bent up, but somehow the car is still running. I called my mom and told her what happened. Then I drove all the way to the YMCA to work out. Dre used to always make fun of my car anyway, but he started laughing when he saw it that morning. Not for humiliation, but kind of like, "Did you still drive out here? You are serious!"

Dre studied the books of Tim Grover, a trainer who worked with players like Michael Jordan, Kobe Bryant, LeBron James, and Dwyane Wade. In those books, he talks about how important it is to still train during the season to prevent injuries, to keep the muscle memory in your body going. That's why we kept doing core workouts during the season, even if I had a game that day.

When it came game time, my muscle endurance was in a whole other space. In the fourth quarter when everybody else was tired, I'm still like, "Let's go!" My body became used to it. Those small, day-to-day practices helped separate me. It wasn't like I grew six more inches. It was the day-to-day habits that we created that helped me separate. I'm going through the season performing at such a high tier. At this point, I have been putting the work in for two or three months, so when it was time to perform on the court, it was just another casual day in the lab.

Toward the end of one practice, after doing play breakdown, Coach Bond called the whole team over and told us, "Oh, I got some good news today." We were all kind of looking at him, ready to go home. He said, "Miss Kim just texted me about Dee's ACT scores." Everybody turned to look at me, and he said, "You finally got that 18 you've been trying to get." The whole team just erupted because they knew I had taken it several times. Even though I still had no college offers, it was a huge feeling of accomplishment, because now, at this point I knew that when one did come, I could get accepted.

Midway through my senior season, Coach Bond still was hard on me, but those chains started to break. He started to trust in my performance. I might break free from a play call and try to do my own thing, and if it didn't work out, he had more patience because he had seen me achieve it a few times. Had I stopped trying to push through when he was hard on me, those chains never would have broken. I had to believe in myself, to keep pushing myself, and it ended up winning him over. When the going gets hard, go harder, and eventually you will prove yourself.

When I'd have to be at the YMCA at 5 a.m., a lot of times I would stay at my friend Tyler's house because he lived closer. We started out as teammates in our sophomore year, and he invited me to go to Panama City, Florida, with his family. From that point forward, that's been my dog. I always felt comfortable around him. He and his family opened the doors of their home to me whenever I wanted to come over. They would always look out for me when they could, whether it was monetary things, or just me going in the fridge and making me a meal.

When I first met Tyler's family, I thought it was an interesting dynamic simply because he was a white guy, and a black man used to always pick him up from practice. Tyler's stepdad grew up in the inner city of South Nashville. Before his success story, he was exactly who I was. He grew up with just his mom, so we could relate. As it turns out, his stepdad and my dad were basketball rivals in high school, playing on opposing teams. When he told me he went to McGavock High School, I said, "Well, my family went to Maplewood." Because Maplewood and McGavock were in the same conference, he's like, "Who your people?" I said, "My daddy graduated in '90. Last name Butler." He said, "Hannibal?" They had already treated me well, but from then on, I was like another son to them.

Tyler believed in me and he believed in my gift. However, by mid-season of my senior year, I'm still not having any colleges scholarship offers. We saw all these players around the city getting the recognition that I wasn't getting, even though I would dominate them when we played their team. Meanwhile, Dre informed me about the importance of getting eligible with the NCAA clearinghouse. He said I would have to fill out all this paperwork online to even be recruited. After we did that, Dre put the idea in my head to start marketing myself by contacting coaches. He'd tell me, "Nobody's going to go as hard for you as you will for yourself."

So, that's what I started doing. My boy Tyler was like, "What do you need me to do?" By midseason, I had some current stats and a highlight reel ready to send, so we stayed up late one night in his family's bonus room and sent off my basketball résumé to 250 coaches—even the coaches where I probably had no chance at playing at their university. You could go to the athletics page of these universities and find the email addresses for the person you were trying to contact. Tyler's on the desktop and I'm on the laptop copying and pasting the same message, sending it everywhere. Flooding emails.

The next morning I'd be checking my emails on the school computer, trying to see if anybody responded to me. Day after day, nothing. I kept up hope though. I had to maintain this firm mindset of still going to practice and still believing that something's going to happen.

Finally, I received three responses. Clemson told me that they weren't interested. They were done recruiting for that upcoming season. Radford told me they were done recruiting in my position; they didn't need any more guards. And the University of Tennessee at Martin told me that they appreciated me reaching out, saying something like, "We would like to stay in touch with you."

And the rest? Nothing. No "Thanks." No "Video received." Straight neglect. No response at all.

So, my senior season's going on and I'm doing my thing, still balling, having a good time. Except for the two or three seniors, we had everybody from the year before, including a big man who was about 6'6". He was a force. But midway through the season, he landed in trouble with the law, ended up put out of school for a while and obviously got kicked off the team. Gone! Again, we were projected to go to state tournament and we just lost our only big man.

Meanwhile, my trainer was still boosting me at the end of the day, like, "That matters, but it don't matter. You built your strength to carry this team over the hump." That was one of those situations where detrimental things happen, and you can either come together or go further apart. One of the two is going to happen, but you're not going to say the same. Our team rallied behind that. From that point on, we lost maybe one or two games, not many.

We started balling out of control and we won our first district tournament game against Portland, Tennessee, which advanced us to the semifinals to play Beech High School. Beech then defeated us in a nailbiter and left us to battle for third seed against Mt. Juliet, our crosstown rival. When we defeated Mt. Juliet in that consolation game, we moved into regionals with our first game against Dickson County High School. They had a very good point guard, a junior who had already committed to Virginia Commonwealth University. The losing team of this matchup would conclude their season, so the road to the state tourney had just gotten more intense.

Keep in mind I still had no college offers and here I am about to go up against one of the best players in the state! Another opportunity to prove myself. We played extremely well that game and went on to defeat Dickson County. When we advanced to regional semifinals, we had to go against Beech High School again. Beech was in the same district as us, so we already played them twice in regular season, and then a week earlier in the district tournament, and now we're lining up one last time. We were tired of seeing them, but they were merely another team in our way of the state tournament. Whoever lost this game, their season would be over.

Beech was notorious for running a defense called a 1-3-1 defense. Up by 30, down by 30, they did not come out of this defense. This was their brand. And if you weren't careful, it was very hard to beat. They were very successful with this. They had us down, I don't remember exactly by how much, but they were on track to win the game. This was do or die.

Even though our big man wasn't there, and Beech was locked in on not letting me beat them single-handedly, we had a freshman come alive this game. We all knew that Jacob Williams had a bright future ahead once his time came, and here it was. He stepped up majorly. I'm talking about he shot the lights out, scoring 20-something points, and it pushed us over the hump to beat Beech in the semifinals. Now we could breathe a little, because with that win, we secured our spot in substate. After lost the regional championship to Clarksville High School, we still had a shot at playing in the state tournament if we won the sub-state game against Brentwood High School on their home court.

Brentwood had a point guard by the name of Jack Montague who was committed to play college basketball at Yale University. Again, another opportunity for me to prove myself as I fought for college exposure. Jack was receiving basketball skills training from a Vanderbilt University basketball great known as Mario Moore. Mario and Dre went to high school together and knew each other fairly well. Now it was time for their prodigies to go against each other.

Wilson Central had a notorious student section called the Blue Zoo. Brentwood was also known for its student section, so we had a battle in the bleachers that game. Brentwood had a very small gym and I could see Mario on the front row of the stands. Dre gave me the rundown on Mario and Jack, and how pretty much Mario thought Jack is the best thing in the world. Here is that rebellious mindset being activated again, like, "We're going to see about that." I'm already ignited, going into this game like, "Oh, yes sir!" I just recall, every time I got a bucket, every time I scored, I'm giving a look over at Mario. Dre's a very arrogant guy as well, so he's shouting at me, like, "They can't hold you! They can't hold you! Go at him!"

I don't know if Coach Bond was nervous himself but he took the backseat and let me rock out. He could tell there was a connection going on in the stands, even though he didn't say one thing about it. It's like he was watching the show. One thing about me is, when I get in my zone and when I get to feeling myself, it's going to be a long night. I play off that adrenaline. That trash talk gets me going. Now that I look back on that game, it's crazy to see how that situation came full circle from Coach Bond saying, "You better do what I say," to him thinking, "Just let him be him." He trusted me. So, sure enough, we ended up eliminating Brentwood. I think I ended that game with about 24, 25 points. I'm doing news interviews after the game, the gym's going crazy, and I remember coming out of the locker room and just hugging Dre. What he was saying from the gate was unfolding right before my eyes: "I'm going to have you in the state tournament."

Mind you, still no college offers. No other replies. And I'm still updating colleges, "Hey, advancing to the state tournament, just following up with you guys..."

The state tournament is held at Middle Tennessee State University, and the depth perception of a college arena is just so different. Shooting at a goal with a wall behind it is much different than shooting at a goal with bleachers behind it. A majority of college gyms are designed like a bowl with seats all the way around the whole arena. So, the rim looks much farther than what it would be if there's a wall behind it, which is how high school gyms are built. As a result, your whole perception is off. A lot of times, if you see guys play a high school game in a college gym, the shots will be short. They'll hit the front rim, or they may even shoot it a lot harder over the rim, because you've got to get used to the depth perception.

Coach Bond had a relationship with Tennessee Tech in Cookeville, so the team went there to practice and to get familiar with playing in a college arena roughly a week before we would tip off at the state tournament. Coach pulled me aside prior to that and said that the Tennessee Tech coaches would be watching me. "This is a good time for you to showcase your ability," he said. "They know about you." Although they weren't recruiting me, they knew about me.

So, we go up there to scrimmage against a team from the Crossville area and I'm trying to really show myself. We're probably 10 minutes into the scrimmage and I get a fast break. The defender is on my hip, trying to slow me down, and when I go up with a layup, I step on his foot. BAM! I fall fast. Coach Bond sprints onto the court and yells, "What's going on? Talk to me!" I'm rolling around and gripping my ankle with both hands as tight as I can, screaming, "MY ANKLE!! ... MY ANKLE!!" I didn't have a lot of ankle sprains that season. I might have tweaked it here and there, but not this severe. I couldn't put any pressure on it. We were seven days out from playing at state and you could see that look of panic in his face.

I was taken back to the training room to put some ice on my ankle. Every 10 minutes, Coach Bond asks me how I'm feeling. And the way I felt was disappointed. I didn't get to perform like I wanted to. I'm done for the rest of the scrimmage. I can't even get out there and show what I'm capable of. The head coach of Tennessee Tech came back there to talk to me. He informed me that he had been watching me during tournament play and to keep doing what I had been doing. That was inspiring to hear, but still I felt like, "Man, that could have been my opportunity."

Coach Bond is talking to our team's physical trainer, asking him, "What are we going to do?" And the trainer's like, "He'll be all right." His name was James. My man, James Tapier. He's very even-keeled all the time. Coach Bond texted me all night with different remedies. He sent me something about Zija, a natural roots mixture that you put in your water. It turns your water brown, and it looks like lake water, but it's supposed to be very good for inflammation, or for anything that's swollen or in pain. He brought some Zija to practice the next morning and forced me drink three bottles of it a day. I'm talking about a terrible taste. But he said, "Just trust me."

Early every morning, leading up to the game, I would meet James for rehab at the school. I could tell he didn't know if I'd be ready for state either, but he was doing everything he could to make it happen. For a couple days I couldn't walk on it, period. I couldn't put pressure on it. He had me in a boot.

He'd put my foot in a cold bath. We did resistance bands. Anything to try to get movement back. While the team was at practice, I would be trying to do different exercises to get my mobility back. Then I would come back every afternoon for another session of rehab. We were doing this three times a day for the next five days.

By Tuesday afternoon on the soccer field, I was able to start back jogging. Even though James didn't ever show a lot of emotion, I noticed him smiling. He was like, "OK, we got a chance." So, now that I'm jogging, I'm feeling more confident and putting more pressure on my ankle. I'm still feeling the pain, but it's healed enough to where I can move a little bit. James tells Coach Bond that I'm jogging at three-quarter speed. Coach is like, "Really? That's fast!"

By the way, Coach Bond is a badass. He used to tell us stories about when he played at Tennessee State University, and at the time he was the only white guy on the team. They called him White Tiger. He said one time when he got his nose busted, he would wipe the blood off, lick the blood, and just keep playing. It didn't surprise me when he expected me to toughen up.

I'm doing some physical therapy at home, so the ankle's getting better over time, but it's still not healed. On Wednesday, I tried to practice a little bit. I finally had some movement to where I could jump and I could move around, but I still wasn't at a hundred percent. Coach said to everybody in practice, "I'm telling you now, if any of you foul Dee during practice, your ass won't be on this damn team next year." In other words, tread lightly.

So here comes Thursday. The state tournament at MTSU. We were set to play Science Hill, a team out from East Tennessee. I took three or four ibuprofen and James taped my ankle so thick that it couldn't move if it wanted to. For me, getting back on the court was mainly a mind thing. My mental fortitude was tough enough to where I wasn't going to let it stop me. This goes back to the night I texted Dre, asking myself, "What have you got to lose?" Even if your ankle falls off, you are going to go out and leave it on the line. I still have no college offers, so it's mandatory that I play.

When the adrenaline kicked in and I got locked into that game, I didn't even think about the ankle. I was moving an inch slower than usual, but my shot was on the money that day. It was like I couldn't miss. When the pain pills kicked in and the adrenaline was running, the ankle was a non-factor. I'm getting up and down the court to the best of my ability. We're playing well, up seven points with a minute and 30 seconds left in the game and getting ready to advance to the next round of state. The college arena atmosphere is crazy. Multiple college coaches, everything you could want as a high school student who wanted to take it to the next level.

Our team's problem was, we weren't playing to win. We were playing not to lose. Instead of just playing the game the rest of the way out, we were being extra conservative, trying to stall the ball a little bit. So, before you know it, Science Hill comes down the court... Bang! A three. Now with the lead cut to four, they give us the full court press. One of our guys is dribbling down but gets trapped in the corner. He tries to step through the trap to pass, but Science Hill steals the ball. They break out. Bang! Another three. Suddenly we're up one point with probably 40 seconds to go. Coach Bond calls timeout. Now we're in panic mode.

Back on the court, we draw an inbound play and we end up getting a breakout on the inbound. The star freshman from the Beech High game ends up being wide open on the inbound. My teammate passes him the ball, he catches it, and takes it all the way down—and misses a layup. It looks like a foul, but the referee calls nothing. Science Hill grabs the ball, comes back down... Bang! Another three. We're down two with seconds left. We come down and try to take a quick shot and miss. Now we're having to foul to stop the clock. At the free throw line, they make three buckets and we end up losing by five. All of this happened in a minute and 30 seconds. The gym is going wild and I'm watching it all fall apart right before my eyes.

In the locker room, we're all shedding silent tears. I'm not knowing what's next. I did make it to the All-Star game that year. My ankle was jacked but I played anyway. Then, about three days later, Tyler, a few more teammates and myself decided to ride down to Panama City for spring break to celebrate our senior year. While I was down there, I got a phone call from UT Martin letting me know that they watched me at the state tournament and that they liked what they saw. I gave them the whole rundown of my ankle and said I didn't really feel like I was at my best. And their coach told me, "We've been keeping up with you. We know what you're capable of."

Then he asked me, "Who is recruiting you at this time?" I was caught by surprise, and I mentioned that I'd been in conversation with a few schools, but I didn't have any offers. And he said, "Well, I want you to consider this your first Division I offer."

I quickly put the phone on mute and looked at Tyler, wanting to shout but instead I'm just stunned. It was like an adrenaline rush of excitement going off on the inside, like I just hit the lottery. I can imagine this is what I will feel when my dad returns home from prison. Then I turned off the mute and said, "I'm sorry, Coach. The phone connection broke up. What did you say?" And as fast as I could, I put it on speakerphone so we could both hear the coach say it: "I want you to consider this your first Division I offer." I'm keeping my composure on the phone, but inside I'm going nuts! Then he says, "We want to get you down here on campus as soon as we can, to show you around, show you how we do things, and see what you'd be interested in."

Later on that same trip, 18 years old and drunk on the beach, I got a call from Alabama A&M. They wanted to get me on campus too. They liked what they saw at the state tournament and gave me an offer as well. So, now I've got two Division I offers. Back home after spring break, I received interest and heavy mail from Youngstown State and Miami University in Ohio. Now things are starting to roll in. The power of never giving up!

I went to visit UT Martin on April 5, but I didn't work out with the team that day. My ankle still wasn't better and playing on it made it worse, so I just watched. Then they toured me around campus and I'm seeing everything. This is my first college visit ever. No idea what to expect. To me, this is all like being recruited by the University of Kentucky. I'm thinking, "This is my chance. This is it. It's everything I've worked for."

UT Martin is part of the Ohio Valley Conference, which was getting a lot of publicity at the time with one of its other teams, Murray State in Kentucky. They were making a national run, doing extremely well, beating major teams and ranked Top 15 in the country. Murray State had a guy named Isaiah

Canaan, who was getting ready to go to the NBA, which was a big deal for that conference. Also, back in 2009, UT Martin had a guy by the name of Lester Hudson who got drafted by the Boston Celtics. The coach still used that as a recruiting pitch: "You know, you remind me of Lester…." I'm falling for all that. It's like, desperate times calls for desperate measures. They had me in a vulnerable spot. Anything you tell me, I'm going to believe it.

I'm so overwhelmed that I commit on the spot. I'm telling them, "You ain't got to worry about it, I'm coming." But we couldn't announce anything until National Signing Day which was April 11, when we staged an official event in my high school library. And that was big, not only because of my story leading up to it, not only because I was the all-time leading scorer in my high school, but because nobody at Wilson Central had ever played Division I basketball. Nobody. One of the players on the women's team also signed to UT Martin, so we had our signing day together.

Granted, the men's team at UT Martin was terrible. I mean, the year before I signed, they had only won four games. I can't remember how many they lost. They were 0-16 in the conference. I had the mindset that I was going to change that. When I signed, people would ask, "How did they do last year?" and I would say it don't even matter. Dre was looking like, "I told you. Just stick to the script." He knew that when I went off to college, I wouldn't be able to be with him as much, but he had prepared me. He had done his part in establishing the foundation. I could take what we had done together and carry it with me to a new location.

6

MAMBA MENTALITY

I didn't know what a big university looked like. So, for me UT Martin was just like... "Wow!" I remember being impressed by the fact that they had a food court with Chick-fil-A, and a couple other little restaurants in there, and you could go to it any time of the day. I'm like, "It's right here on campus? I could just walk to it?" And the main cafeteria had such a variety too. The truth is, I've always been infatuated with choices. I'm still that way. I love to feel the freedom of having choices, of having options.

You hear all these stories, all these experiences, myths, and party stories about college, but to walk on campus and see it gives you a completely different feeling. I'm going in the dorms and seeing that these guys basically have their own apartment, living on their own. No chaperones. You're here on campus with a bunch of other people your age with no parents around. That itself was like, "OK, that sounds dope."

I didn't take my old Nissan Sentra up there, so I never strayed too far off campus during my freshman year. The nearest shopping mall was 50 miles away, in Jackson, Tennessee. Or you could go to Paducah, Kentucky. Those were the nearest places to find a pair of shoes or an outfit. We had to go 20 minutes to Union City, Tennessee, to even get a nice sit-down restaurant, which was Applebee's. Everything in Martin was mainly fast food. And we had Walmart, which was the hub for everybody on campus. That's where you went to buy groceries, electronics, home necessities, etc.

As a way to get some hours rolling, I enrolled in summer school. That way I wouldn't have to overwhelm myself during basketball season. Instead, I could just take the mandatory hours I needed to stay eligible. Summer school got me accustomed to campus life before everything got overwhelming, and it allowed me to start getting involved in workouts, getting on the weights, skill work, and just the overall transition into college. The biggest thing that people have to understand, when you're on a college team, is that everybody there was the man on their high school team. Playing at the college level thins out the lesser talent, and as you get to the pros, it gets even thinner. But nobody on this team would be here if they didn't dominate on their high school team.

I only knew one person on campus, a guy from Memphis that I played AAU ball against. Outside of that, I didn't know anybody. Unsurprisingly I wasn't nervous about taking on this new challenge that was drawing so much attention from peers, relatives and strangers. I've never been afraid of attention. Never in my life. Hence, the class clown. Now my confidence was better, but it still wasn't where it needed to be to perform at a high level, on the collegiate level, because this was still unfamiliar turf. I had never done anything like it. Three months before getting here, I didn't even have an offer. It took a while for my mind to really catch up to the fact that I am now a Division I college athlete.

It helped that there wasn't a huge expectation, considering the team sucked. I didn't go to a team that was used to achieving greatness, even though I was a champion at heart. I kept that championship mindset. That began to show a few weeks into being on campus, simply because I would do things like get in the gym on off days. Stay after practice and get up shots. Ask coach for extra workouts. I'm doing this as a college freshman because that's what was instilled in me in high school.

One day, our head coach Jason James pulled me in his office for a conversation. He was telling me, "We don't have a leader. That's the reason why this team is in the predicament that it's in. We don't have anybody on our team that leads by example, on the floor and off the floor. I can tell you come from a good foundation at home, so I don't have to worry about you acting an ass off the court."

He also told me, "Don't shy away from leadership because you're young. Let your everyday habits do the talking." He's not saying to come in here, be vocal, talk crazy. Because I'm asking him, "Do you think these guys will listen to me as a freshman?" He said, "Just lead by example and it'll gradually happen. You're doing all the right things." The fact that he even presented that conversation gave me another layer of confidence.

Coach James and the team nominated me for SAAC, which stands for Student Athletic Advisory Committee. At these meetings, we'd talk about rules, regulations, and policies that affect all the student athletes. You normally have two representatives from each sports club. Again, this goes back to that leadership role. Coach felt that I was a good representation of the team, so they put me on the advisory board. I think that was his way of pushing me into that leadership role for the team to see it as well. That was his way of not vocalizing it, but showing it by actions, saying, "OK, this is the guy that's going to vouch for us." I was shocked that they put me on it because I'd only been on campus for a year, so I didn't have a lot of experience. But at that age, I could speak well. I was articulate. I knew how to have a conversation with people.

The guys that I hung around on a day-to-day basis were all upper-classmen, juniors and seniors. They never wanted to get in the gym. Outside of practice, they were in the dorm with the women, kicking it. As a freshman I got caught up in that sometimes, because I'm new on campus, still an 18-year-old boy. I'm in that transitional phase in life of searching for my identity. Who am I really? What do I really like to do, now that I'm not under mama's armpit anymore? Now that I'm making my own decisions, what am I really interested in?

I've always gravitated to older people. However, I saw myself falling into the things that these older people were falling into, because I was always around these guys. They're slowly shaping my identity. They're not even aware of it. I'm a natural leader, but I was in a follower state because I was in unfamiliar territory. I'm trying to learn how to navigate my way through. I would get caught up in things like late nights and drinking. We'd be up all night, kicking it with the volleyball team, kicking it with the soccer team. Distractions.

This is how my teammates operated in their college time, which is why the season record was what it was.

My mental fortitude wasn't as strong as it needed to be at the time, so I realized I would have to stay away from them to stay focused. That was a challenge within itself, going against the norm of what everybody was doing. They didn't know how my coach's meetings went, but behind closed doors, Coach James is telling me that he could see me being the next guy with his jersey in the rafters. I'm trying to live up to that expectation. I don't know what it takes to get there, but I do know that I'm trying to lock in and do that.

At the same time, I'm still the kid that comes from everything I've told you about in chapters one through five. That was an everyday battle because the coach is telling me I got potential. Meanwhile, I don't know if I believe that I have it, and I thoroughly enjoy the social life that comes with being in college. For me, the battle was the discipline of staying committed to doing things that were uncomfortable. Going to sleep early so I can wake up early. Getting to practice early, when I know my teammates aren't coming in for another hour and a half. Staying later after practice when everybody else is about to get ready to get lit tonight. In reality I wanted to be partying, but I'm looking at the bigger picture. In order to get to where you want to go, in order to get somewhere you never been, you've got to do things you've never done. And that takes extreme discipline. I admit that I fell short at times.

Another thing that made it hard is that we were losing so many games. I'm spending this extra time in the gym and we'd still get beat by 40. As a freshman, I really wasn't getting that much playing time like I thought I should have been. But stick to the script. Stick to the script. You still need to show up, even when things aren't going the way you expect them to be going. You still need to perform your task to the best in your capabilities.

As humans, we're not smart enough to predict the future. I wish we were, but we're not. However, you can impact the future. You can do things daily that improve your chances for certain outcomes or lessen your chances for certain outcomes. It is about preparing your field. It's not about the instant result. It's about the process over time. It's important to just stay in the moment and show up every day looking to get one percent better. Practice by practice, game by game. It's about improving. It doesn't happen in a night. Just because you lose, you don't throw the whole experience away. Coach James would always say, "We have bad moments, not bad days." Something's pissing you off? You had a bad moment. Your whole day's not bad, you just had a bad moment. Don't let a moment of dissatisfaction ruin the entire thing.

There were two nightclubs in Martin. You had one where your black people went, and one where the white people went. It sounds crazy, but this was just reality. You had a rodeo-style, cowboy-boots, hole-in-the-wall bar called Cadillacs, and you had Cheers, which had nightclub scenery and a live DJ. That's where all the Divine Nine African American sororities and fraternities went. That's where all your black people went. These clubs were three minutes apart.

For my first party, I remember going to Cheers and having the time of my life. That was my first time being around African American women that I felt an attraction to. My community back home was so small, the black women at school were mostly relatives. And if not, I never did really have any interactions with them. So, I'm seeing them at UT Martin and I'm like, "OK!"

I had this one black girl in my math lab, and from day one, she had it out for me. I don't know if it was because she could see that I was an athlete. As a freshman, I always went to class in jumpsuits, hoodies, sweats, or something athletic-related. I never put regular clothes on. She just had it out for me, man. It was that "tough love" kind of flirting. She was always talking trash. That was her way to start conversation. We're already in a math lab, to get help outside of math class, and she asked me if I could help her with some of her work outside of class. She wanted to schedule some "study time." So, numbers were exchanged, and she ended up coming over to my dorm with her folder as if this was the real intent. And man, one thing led to another, and that was my first time ever seriously having deeper-level intimacy with a black girl.

After I'd done it, I remember telling my mom like it was a proud moment: "I hooked up with this girl and she was black." My family predicted that I would be with white women for the rest of my life. Not that they had a problem with it, but Mom was like, "For real?" It was definitely a response of shock. And a relief because she does always jokingly say that she wants black grandbabies. Anyway, we didn't have too much conversation about it because it's still my mama I'm talking to!

That's around the time when I started tapping into my inner self more. I'm starting to appreciate and like the skin that I was in. That population at UT Martin is very diverse. There were a lot of black people. My team was all black with the exception of one player. I went from playing on basically all-white high school teams to a college team where we had one white guy. The head coach was black. The assistants were black, except for one assistant coach who was white. The roles had flipped.

We had a guy from New Orleans, we had guys from Memphis, guys from Little Rock, Arkansas. We had a guy from St. Louis. A guy from Virginia, a guy from Akron, Ohio. We had a guy from Cameroon, Africa. Just a lot of cultures in one area. And the funny thing about college is, your team never stays the same. Your team changes every year. Guys drop out of college, guys transfer, new guys are signed on scholarship, freshmen are coming in, guys are coming in from junior college. The locker room culture is re-identifying, year after year.

Being around black teammates, I was getting exposed to more things, like slang terminology and even fashion. I think it's an unspoken rule that black people's fashion and white people's fashion are polar opposites. The interests are just different. I grew up around predominantly white people, so whatever I had on was acceptable to them. They didn't know any better. What I mean by that is, if I got on a fake pair of Jordans or real pair of Jordans, they don't know. Whereas in the black community, that's a big deal. Your reputation is based on what you wear.

I remember hearing about a guy named J-Dubb on my first visit to campus. Even when I was in summer school, one of my teammates was like, "I can't wait until you meet Dubb. Y'all going to hit it off." I'm like, "Who is this dude?" And when we met, we did hit it off. My boy. I spent a vast majority of my time with him when I was a freshman and he was a senior. They called him the granddaddy of the team because he was 26 years old. He didn't start college until he was 22. He became a big brother to me. He took me in as the younger brother.

Unfortunately, he was the guy who was always the ringleader of partying. The ringleader of doing everything instead of getting in the gym. But this is my dog, this is my boy. He always said I'm a little brother he never had, because he's the baby of his siblings. People always say we acted alike, but unlike J-Dubb, I didn't have any taste for fashion. When I go back and look at pictures now, I'm like, "What in the hell was I wearing?"

We tailgated at every home football game as a team. I've always been a joker, so I'm joking on Dubb all day at the time for whatever reason. I don't know what made him decide to do it, but he looked down at my shoes and he saw a color on my Jordans that he didn't remember being on that shoe. I had the knockoffs. And while I was giving him a hard time, he told one of our other homeboys, "Hey, Google that Jordan right there. Let me see how it looks." He's saying this on the side. I'm not hearing him at the time.

So, Dubb sees the real picture of what my shoe was supposed to look like, and for the next 45 minutes, he made that moment about me! Joking the whole time, making fun of me. Everybody's laughing. It's funny, but it's embarrassing too, and from that day forward, I never bought another pair of fake Jordans. Never in my life. I'm like, "Nah, this is never happening to me again." I was already dealing with insecurities, and here I am getting roasted for my apparel. That's when my mind got washed into thinking that your outer appearance defines you. I was suddenly more conscious about what I had on. It got even worse the next year, my sophomore year.

That's when my body started to change. Put a little more weight on and grew a little bit stronger. I had a good summer prior to my sophomore year. Stayed on campus but came home for maybe a month. I met up with Dre for workouts and he's still pumping into me, "These guys ain't doing what you're doing." I'm knowing that at this time because I just finished a year up there. I know they ain't putting in that extra effort. They're at home kicking it.

I'm at home grinding, getting back to our regular regimen, getting up in the morning on the resistance bands, doing skill work, then doing cardio. Dre is strengthening my mind and strengthening my body as this is going on.

When I go back to college for summer school in July, other guys are coming back from vacationing for two months. I'm in tip-top shape. I'm competing. My mind is in a different mode. My confidence is better because I already know what a college season consists of. I'm already aware of what kind of teammates I have. We were all looking forward to a better year, because the first year we went 8-23. That summer I started separating myself a little bit. Started playing better. We had some transfers coming in who were supposed to be very good, so I had connected with them via social media. This is how my friend Marshun Newell got introduced.

Remember when I was being recruited, my coach was telling me how I could be the next Lester Hudson? Now going into my sophomore year, they're telling me they're getting ready to sign Lester's cousin. They're telling me all about Marshun, and they were like, "There's one hiccup about him. He's freshly out of jail." At that point, we're all like, "Who the hell are we bringing up in here?"

We had his name so we started Googling him in the locker room, trying to figure out who's getting ready to be on our team. He had come down to visit over the summer when nobody was there, except for two guys who said that he was killing them on the court. They were like, "He can play." Because his cousin was in the NBA, we were all happy to draw on that correlation, like, "We might have another Lester." Now we saw the charges and found out he had been facing a lengthy term of years to life in prison. He went to trial and ended up beating the case.

When he gets to campus, he and I clicked immediately. Like very, very, very dope dude. A good genuine guy. He comes from the inner city of Memphis. I'm not sure with how familiar you are with Memphis, but the inner city is rough. Going back to visit his neighborhoods, I built a relationship with his people, his family. He never knew his dad from birth. His mother and his grandmother had both passed away, so he had been raising himself since he was 14 years old. He went to jail in his early 20s, while he was in community college. After a year in jail, he earned a scholarship to play two years at UT Martin. We became very close, so I ended up spending a lot of time in his neighborhood in Memphis. I'm seeing the day-to-day life of a lot of black people in marginalized communities. And I'm thinking, I may have been poor as hell, but I had support.

Learning more about Marshun and his situation made me more appreciative and grateful for my situation. This became a time when my mom and I grew closer too. In my senior year of high school, I had started acting almost like, "I have arrived! There's nothing you can tell me!" Our relationship had gotten rocky a little bit. I was very hard on her. I would undermine everything she would tell me. I'm not understanding that she's dealing with one son who's incarcerated and meanwhile trying to keep the other one in line. But I felt like a shark in a fish tank. I've outgrown this environment. Everybody else is at a standstill, just the same repetitive actions, day in and day out. It seemed as if nobody was trying to expand their life, push the limits, or try new things. My hero, my brother, was in jail, and with my mom, there was no excitement or thrill that she was bringing. In my mind, I thought, "I've maxed myself out here." That mindset was true, but I was showing it in demoralizing ways.

My actions were coming from a hurt place. As I always say, hurt people hurt people. My behaviors were stemming from unresolved issues as a child. Of abandonment, of feeling inadequate, of feeling less than. Feeling like that outlier, of being the black sheep, the black person in a pool full of white people. They were my own internal things, but I would take them out in other ways. I learned that once you know better, you do better. And as I knew better, I became more self-aware and started healing and working on these things. My exterior behaviors became much more positive in how I treated people, and how I valued individuals. My two years at UT Martin were life-altering.

My mom never swayed during this time. She always stayed the same, as far as her support. That never wavered, and that says a lot about her. She never got so caught up in me being ungrateful that she stopped doing things for me. She even told me back in high school, "If you get a full ride to college and you stay out of trouble, I'll get you a new car." Sure enough, when I came home before my sophomore year of college started, she surprised me with a 2012 Nissan Altima.

I had a mom who loved me and a family who cared about me. Not everybody can say that, but I didn't really realize that coming from my own situation. When I got to college, I was exposed to other people's stories and I'm like, "Man, my life could have been way worse." I met other young men whose situations were way worse than what I had, in regards to the lack of support, in regards to the treacherous environments of violence that they had to grow up in.

You know how I talked earlier about how people could see things in me that I couldn't see? These students wanted to come home with me for Thanksgiving, or for the Christmas holidays. They wanted to come to Nashville and I'm like, "Why would they want to do that?" They're gravitating toward my house because they felt like my situation was so much better than what they had. My mama treated them like family. It ended up becoming that type of dynamic. Here I am, thinking that my situation was so piss-poor, but in reality it was somebody else's dream. It made me much more appreciative, much more humble. I mean, I'm a sophomore in college with a brand new car.

Like I said, there was some uncertainty when Marshun first came, because again, I'm looking at his history. But he loved to get in the gym after hours, just like I did. So, that's how it started. We're both putting in extra work together. Our bond ended up getting so close, he wouldn't ride in nobody else's car but mine. His mindset was already different than a typical college student because of what he came from. He dealt with a lot of trust issues. I was that relatable connection for him because I come from rough beginnings and uncomfortable beginnings as well. However, I'm not that inner-city, fast-life kid. I'm giving him a perspective of another life, more of a balanced, levelheaded perspective.

By this time, my boy Dubb had graduated. Marshun took Dubb's place in my life because he was a few years older than me too. What he brought to the table was a ton of life experience because he had to grow up so young. He dealt with so many severe, traumatic situations as a kid. When he took Dubb's spot into being the leader, per se, that was good and bad for me. Based on what he comes from, the mentality's totally different. He was interested in things that I never had interest in, but I gained interest by hanging around him.

When the stuff happened with the fake Jordans, I already had in my mind that how you look and what you wear matters. That if I got on designer brands, that means I got money. Even if I ain't got a pot to piss in, people are going to think I got some money if I'm wearing Gucci, head to toe. That was Marshun's mentality too. He had designer shoes, Gucci belts, all that, and he came from the hood. I always wondered, "How do people in the hood have all this, and don't even got a place to lay their head?" Or, "How do y'all have these shoes that cost $1,200, and y'all ain't even got a car?"

At the time, True Religion was the brand that was very popular. True Religion pants are $200 a pair. Marshun would let you know, like, "Man, if you want to get these girls, you can't be wearing bullshit." And I'm believing it, because I'm going to tell you one thing about him. Boy had a lot of women. That's nothing to pat on the back, but I'm just saying. They would come and visit him from every city in the South and he had some on campus. He was a ladies man. He used to say, "You got to step your swag up." That took me away from my roots. I could hear that voice in my head: "That's not how you were raised. You used to survive on minimum. Now you're thinking you need $200 pants?"

My girlfriend in my sophomore year bought my first pair of True Religion pants. Marshun convinced me to talk her into getting them for my birthday. From that point to when I graduated college, I wouldn't wear no pants unless they were True Religion. I wouldn't put the pants on. It was all mental. I'm not bashing him for it, but that's where I learned that. I started to form this mindset that, if I ain't got this on, I don't even want them. It became my identity for a while.

So now, before I knew it, I had my brother on that type of time. I had my little cousin on that type of time. They're trying to get True Religion because I was telling them, "This is what we're supposed to be in." Then they opened up a True Religion store at a mall in Nashville. Man, I had a closet full of True Religion. I'm spending hundreds of dollars on True Religion like it's nothing.

In college you get Pell Grant checks, and when I'm getting those checks, I'm buying designer clothes. That's how I'm spending my money.

I was really close to the athletic trainer and some other people on campus, and they could see the change in me. They used to tell me, "You need to stop hanging around Marshun." They weren't saying he was a terrible person, but they knew who I was when I got there, and who they saw me become when I was with him. But I couldn't see it. At the end of the day, those are nice things to have, but they mean absolutely nothing. When you don't have an identity, you do what you see. You follow, and that becomes your identity. That's why it's so important to make sure you are surrounded by the right influences.

I had a hell of a sophomore year. We had a scrimmage before the season started and I scored 30-something points with eight three-pointers. Our first two games of the season were part of a road trip against Wyoming and Colorado. Both teams had NBA draft picks. I came out and scored 15 points both games, off the bench. Over the summer, I was preparing for these moments.

Then things started getting shaky with the minutes and play rotation. Performances started to change. I might play 25 minutes here, 10 minutes there. You have 10 to 12 non-conference games before you even get to conference, and it was just up and down. When conference came around, it picked back up and I started killing it again, averaging 10 or 11 points in conference. The problem was that our head coach wasn't consistent. You're only as good as your leader, and he changed the lineup so many times.

When we were playing UNLV, we were down maybe eight points at half time. Our leading scorer on the team, a very good basketball player, was a knucklehead off the court. In trouble all the time, in fights, just a damn head case. He held Coach James hostage. What I mean by that is, Coach knew we needed him on the court, so he didn't hold him to the same disciplinary actions as everybody else. That player would cuss Coach out, talk crazy to him, but Coach felt like he had to play him, in order to give us a chance to win.

During that game in Vegas, Coach subbed this guy during the game. Coach was trying to talk to him while he was coming from court. He just stormed past Coach and sat at the end of the bench. And when he's at the end of the bench, he's shouting things like, "See, look at what they're out there doing! Every time you take me out, the lead goes up!" He's speaking out loud, hoping somebody will say something. You know those people. He was like, "Look, here they go. Now we finna get beat by 30."

At halftime in the locker room, Coach comes in barking. "I just don't know what to do anymore. You guys won't listen. You just do your own thing. Anybody got something they want to say? Y'all seem to have all the answers. What's going on? Y'all tell me." This was the day when I solidified my leadership spot amongst my teammates. Everybody's looking down and I said, "Coach, to be honest, until this team gets some discipline, we're never going to really be good."

After I said this, you could hear pin drop. The assistant coaches went from having their head down to looking right at me. My teammates and I had been talking about this in the dorms like, "Man, Coach allows certain people do whatever they want to do." We all knew it, but nobody would say it to the coach, and now I'm putting him on the spot.

He said, "Oh, you must have all the answers. Discipline? What do you mean, discipline?" And I said, "Just for example, Coach, you're sitting here barking at us about not listening to you or doing what we want to do. I'm not trying to throw anybody under the bus, but when you take certain people out the game, they tell you whatever they want to tell you, and you act like nothing happened." The same thing would happen in practice too. We're all running sprints, and if you don't make the time, you run again. Let's say our big man doesn't make his time. He wouldn't have to do that sprint again. He'd be like, "My knee hurts. I ain't running."

What I said pissed some teammates off. "Motherfuckers need to worry about they self. Everybody worry about what the next person doing" was mumbled under their breath. I'm like, "I'm just being honest. It's been like this since I've been in here. It's my second year. There's no disciplinary actions to anything that's going on."

We only had X amount of time to really talk at halftime, then you're back out to the court. We put a pencil in it and carried on. We came out of the second half and got beat by 30. The energy was just flat. After the game, behind closed doors at the hotel, one of the assistant coaches applauded me for what I said. Unbelievably, they didn't have the courage to say something like that. They talked about it with each other, but nobody ever told Coach James. Nobody ever checked him about it.

From that day forward, even though it pissed a couple teammates off, a majority of them respected my mind. They respected my voice after I took a stand. After that, we started conference play, and I had a very good year in conference that year. Shooting 50 percent from the three-point line, just playing good ball. You're starting to see that the players would feed me the ball more, playing through me to an extent. Not all of them, because some of the players still feel some kind of way. But next year, these seniors that are mad are going to be gone.

Meanwhile, Coach James knew something was up. Later in the season, he would tell us, "Even if it's my last game, I'm going to coach to the end." The way the conference worked in the OVC is, everybody doesn't make it to the conference tournament. You have to place, I think, in the top eight to make it, and we were straddling the line. Long story short, we ended up not making it that year and Coach got fired. They called us all in to let us know what was going on. Some of the assistant coaches were still there working us out while this was happening. One of the assistant coaches told me, "You've had a good year and you need to get out of here. You need to transfer. I don't know who they're going to bring in."

But see, because of the way rules are, you have to sit out a year when you transfer, but you can get that year back. I didn't like that. I was like, "Nah, I want to play." That coach started shopping around for some interest on my behalf, because I wasn't allowed to talk to other schools. He found out that Ole Miss was interested. So were Illinois State and UT Chattanooga.

Ole Miss, now that raised my eyebrows. That's SEC basketball. But it ended up coming back that they wanted me to be able to play right away. They were looking for guys to help come in and win now. It did them no good for me to transfer if I couldn't play. One of the other guys at UT Martin, who had graduated but still had one year left to play, ended up going to Ole Miss. But there was no way I could qualify.

In April, UT Martin announced that our new coach was coming from UNLV, the team that blew our ass out. Coach Heath Schroyer had been that team's assistant coach, and he knew I was the main resource to want to keep. Out of the guys that had the most years left at UT Martin, I was probably the best one. So, he made it his priority to make sure he didn't lose me. On his first day on campus, he took me out to dinner, breaking down why he's so thrilled to be here, how he's watched films of the team, and what he sees in me. It's the recruiting process all over again.

That year, UNLV had the number one NBA draft pick, a guy named Anthony Bennett. Coach Schroyer coached him. That was on his résumé, and I knew that. I knew for sure this coach has the NBA connections. And after the year I had as a sophomore, I'm thinking, "I might have a chance." He's feeding off that. He's giving me all these inside personal stories with some of these draft picks and how the draft works. We don't know about all that at UT Martin, so I'm eating it up. I'm like, "Man, this might really be a dream come true."

He's telling me, "My good friend, he's in the upstairs department for the Orlando Magic. I talk to him every day. I'm going to have these guys coming to practices." He's selling me a pipe dream. He's saying, "My goal is to get you ready to where you're ready for pro day." He said he wanted to get me ready to work out in front of NBA scouts and play in the NBA summer league, which is a showcase held in Las Vegas every summer where guys are competing for NBA contracts. Where I come from, these things are unheard of, so to be having these conversations with a man who has just done this for somebody, it's enticing.

Even though my assistant coaches were telling me that I needed to leave, I'm like, "Y'all ain't hearing what I'm hearing, though." Coach Schroyer knew that I was still on the fence. I told him I was thinking about getting in the transfer portal. Coach Will Wade at UT Chattanooga wanted me to come down and sign, and Illinois State still had an interest. Coach Shroyer even went to the extent of making sure my dorm room stayed full with groceries. He took care of me, and I decided to stay.

At first, Coach Schroyer made it about me. He was intentional about that. Even in summer workouts, he's telling everybody, "Get him the ball. He's our guy." He's telling me he ain't bringing other guys. Then, the first red flag. I remember being at home for the last few days of summer at my aunt's house and she asked me, "Who is Deville Smith?" I'm like, "What do you know about Deville?" She said, "It just came across the ESPN app that he transferred to your school." I picked up my phone and I saw the notification too. I knew who Deville Smith was. I knew his name, just from the circuit of sports. I've been knowing that name for a while.

Deville Smith was a very high-profile player right out of high school. He played point guard at UNLV after spending time at Mississippi State and a junior college. He now was a fifth-year senior who had graduated and had a free year to play. And now I find out on my damn phone that Coach Shroyer is bringing him to UT Martin. I'm happy, but then again, that impacts me a little bit. We share positions.

I texted Coach Shroyer and said, "Hey, we got Deville coming?" He wrote back, "It's not finalized yet, but I'm trying to get him here. I think you and him would be perfect together." That's how he's pitching it. He said, "I've been trying to find you some help in the guard play, so that we can really take this thing to the NCAA tournament." He's still making it sound good, but I can buy those words too, because I know Deville is a good player. I'm like, "Yeah, let's go!"

My junior year season starts off a little rough. You got me, Deville, Marshun, and a couple of other guys that Coach Schroyer brought in, all playing the same position. I'm back competing for minutes again. I'm starting to contemplate regrets but I'm locked in. I'm starting to wonder, "Did I make the right decision? Or did I just fuck my career up?"

For the first couple scrimmages, Coach wasn't really playing me. I got off to a slow start in our first scrimmage against University of Arkansas at Little Rock, and he benched me quick. And it didn't make it any better because when he benched me, he put Marshun in—and Marshun is playing well. That's hard for me because this is my friend. I want to see him do well, but at the same time, we're competing for minutes. We could have been playing alongside each other, but Coach didn't play us like that.

First game of the year was against Marquette. I didn't play very many minutes. We played Arkansas State and I was on the court for one minute. Literally, one minute. At this point, my confidence is rattled. He's playing me on what they call eggshells. One mistake, he's pulling me out. If I miss a shot or take a shot that he doesn't agree with, I'm coming out. It's like you're messing up because you're playing not to mess up. I feel stripped, again, of all confidence. What made it worse was that we're winning games. I couldn't really complain much because it looks terrible when we're winning games and you still aren't happy.

We're six games in and I'm not even feeling like I'm a part of the team, simply because I'm not playing. I go from ending my sophomore season with a bang to just some motherfucker with a jersey. We're 4-2 and heading to Virginia to play Longwood University. I'm playing fairly well in this game, but Coach still has me on a heavy rotation stream. I'm making the most of my minutes, but he's putting me in, pulling me out, putting me in, pulling me out. We end up winning the game, putting us at 5-2. This is the best start in UT Martin history in the past four or five years, and it's with a new coach.

The whole time, even though it's looking promising, I'm pissed. I'm unhappy on the inside. We're in the locker room, everybody's going crazy, and Coach asks me, "Are you not happy? We just won the game." I was like, "Yeah, I'm good." At this point I'm checked out. We had taken a sleeper bus to Virginia, one of those big charter buses with beds, and it was about an 11-hour ride home. When we stopped and got food on the way back, I'm so checked out that I'm not even being social. The only one who knew anything about my frame of mind was Marshun. I told him, "I'm gone, bro." He's like, "Man, you ain't going nowhere, bro." That's what he is telling me. I'm like, "I'm done." But see, I couldn't announce my moves just yet. I could only say, "I don't know where I'm going yet, but I'm leaving."

All the way back to campus from the game in Virginia, I'm on my phone working my plan, texting my boy Tyler, because he was the manager of the UT Chattanooga team. He's already knowing about this situation. When I wanted to transfer at first, he was the one that got Coach Wade involved. And when I told him I was going to stay at UT Martin, it pissed him off a little bit because he wanted me to leave. He knew that I had been unhappy with that decision because we talked every day. He said, "Do you want me to see about coming to UT Chatt?" There was a guy on that team that Coach Wade was talking about maybe transferring. I told Tyler, "Yes, if Coach Wade is still interested, then I am coming. I am done here."

Man, Tyler works fast. That next day was Sunday and we had Sunday off. Tyler calls me and asks, "Can you talk on the phone for a minute?" Coach Wade and I are not supposed to have contact with each other, so Tyler puts me on speaker phone. Coach Wade is telling Tyler it's going to be too hard to file for a medical red shirt, which is an injury that puts you out for the year. Then he says, "But I think we can file with the clearinghouse and get this year back, considering it's only been seven games into the season." I'm hearing this and thinking I'll still have two years to play. He said, "We're going to get you up here. I got you." I said, "Well, tomorrow morning, I'm going to tell Coach Schroyer I'm done and ask for my transfer papers."

I spent all Sunday thinking about it. I go to study hall, it's on my mind. I texted Coach Schroyer that night and said, "Can we meet first thing in the morning?" He said, "Sure thing, no problem." Ain't no turning around now. I'm up until 3 or 4 a.m. Can't sleep. This is the biggest decision of my life because there's uncertainty at Chattanooga too. They were winning games. They didn't need me. That's a good team. I am about to get on a team that is already winning, to prove myself again and hopefully get minutes. It wasn't guaranteed. Coach Wade let me know that. He said, "I'm going to treat you fair, and this is going to be the best you've ever been taken care of, but it's also going to be the hardest you've ever worked."

Monday morning comes. I end up going into the meeting and I'm nervous. I just wanted to get out. Even walking over there, I'm texting Tyler the whole time, prepping my conversation. I'm doing role-playing because I don't want to get in there and not be able to talk. It's early morning and Coach has his hair all gelled up, like he's fresh out of the shower. That's how he used to wear his hair. All gelled up and spiked, all day. I'm like, "What's up, coach?" He said, "Close the door."

For some reason that always makes it even more intense when you close the door. Then he's like, "What's going on? Talk to me." I was like, "Coach, I'm not here to really ask for permission. I'm not really here to negotiate. I'm here more so to inform." That's exactly what I said. Then I told him, "The things that you and I discussed when you first took the job, about my goals and my personal goals, and what you saw for me -- that is not what's currently taking place."

I can see how that could be perceived as vague, and Coach says, "What do you mean? What are you saying?" I said, "I'm barely getting minutes. What you and I discussed is not what's going on." And he said, "What do you want, to transfer? Do you want to leave?" I said, "I think it's come to that point."

His face turned red. He asked me, "So, instead of working your butt off and competing for minutes, you want to leave? We're 5-2! The school's never done that. And you want to jump ship? Where do you want to go? Chattanooga?" I said, "Coach, I ain't even thought that far ahead. I just know that I do want a different location and I need time to just clear my mind." And then I said, "It's going to be somewhere closer to home, though. Maybe Division II." And he was like, "You sure that this is for sure what you want to do?" I said, "It is."

He looked right at me. "OK, well, I'll speak with the athletic director and we'll see about getting the papers. Let's meet back this afternoon. Let's spend some more time thinking about this."

Not even two hours later, a text came in from the assistant coach: "You going to leave for real, man?" I guess they just had a coaches meeting when I left. I wrote back, "I got to." He asked me to meet him in the parking lot. When he came outside, we were just talking casually. He wasn't being an advocate, saying I should stay. He was just telling me, as a player, no matter where you go, you've got to be mentally tough. If things aren't going how you want them to go, the way to handle it is not necessarily to get up and quit to go somewhere else. He said, "Wherever you go, you've got to have that mindset. If you can go out and get the best situation somewhere else, do it. But most importantly, your mind has got to get stronger. You know I want the best for you, so whether you're here or whether you're somewhere else, there's still going to be problems."

At about 2 p.m., I went back to Coach Schroyer's office. He asked me again, "So this is what you want do?" At this point, the conversation is easier. I said, "Yes, I'm done." He said, "When you finish your exams Wednesday, just go ahead and pack your stuff. We'll move forward from this and put it behind us. I'll take care of the rooming situations."

When I told Marshun, he said, "Man, you really going to leave? That's crazzzy." I'm like, "Bro, I'm gone, man. I can't just let my career dwindle down like this. If it don't work out, it don't work out, but it isn't going to be because I didn't try."

Immediately after my finals on Wednesday, I drove a few hours west to Jonesboro, Arkansas, where Dubb was living. After clearing my mind at Dubb's place, I left early Friday morning to drive back to Martin for an eye doctor appointment. Christmas Break had started, so there was not too much going on. Then, right after that appointment, I set off with my car jam-packed with everything from my dorm. Next stop: Lebanon, Tennessee, to my mama's house.

7
VISITATION ROOM

We always eat a family breakfast at Christmas, along with exchanging gifts and just spending time together. And for the past two decades, I can't ever recall my dad being there for Christmas. When I was young, he would come by on Christmas Day. He'd probably swing by later in the afternoon with more gifts, but I wouldn't ever wake up and unwrap gifts with my dad. I've never experienced that in my life.

My relationship with my dad has been strictly cultivated through phone calls, visitation rooms and letters. That's how our relationship has been built. I don't have that experience of going out in the backyard playing catch, throwing the baseball with my dad, or learning how to throw a football, or having him teach me how to play basketball. These are all sports that he played but I don't have the experience of him walking me through those steps to teach me.

I've seen that and I've done that with other people's dads. Maybe I've been over at their house and we're out running routes and their dad plays the quarterback. Or even something as simple as being at a friend's house and his dad is sitting in the garage while we're playing basketball in the driveway. He's watching, commentating, whatever. Those things seem small but they're actually self-esteem builders. It's another way of feeling supported, just being seen. Feeling valued, with somebody caring about you. Like I said, I always had to experience that through phone calls, letters, and the short amounts of time I would get in the visitation rooms.

Before I could drive, I could only go see my dad whenever it fit my mom's schedule or my grandma's schedule. They're balancing multiple things themselves, so it wasn't often that I could go to visitation. We would try to make a trip around the holidays, maybe on school break, but I didn't have control of that. It's just whenever we got time. Before he transferred to a closer location that is now three and a half hours away, my dad was in a federal prison in Ashland, Kentucky, for some years and that's about a six-hour drive. My mom took me a couple times to see him while he was incarcerated there, but it was hard on my grandma to drive six hours straight, with all my cousins and me in the car, and then turn around and drive six hours back.

For somebody in prison, visitation and phone calls are what helps them do their time. Laying their eyes on you can really help them get through the next six months. It's crazy to think about that, but that's the reality. People spending time in prison needs the love and connection from the outside world, without a doubt, from their family! However, it is a very traumatic experience being a visitor at a prison, especially when you're going to see a loved one, such as a parent, or if it's a parent going to see a child. Let me tell you what that looked like for me as a kid.

I've seen my dad in all of the phases. I've seen him in county jail, where I had to talk to him through a glass window on a phone. I could see him but not touch him, so that right there is traumatic. It's like having something in a glass case, something that you're trying to get to, and you can't. It's impossible. It's almost like dangling bait.

When he got his sentence and went to prison, visitations became different. These visitations have contact. My dad got to physically come out and sit down. There are food vending machines so you can eat meals together. But you've got to pay for them, so you bring coins in. These are meals they don't get back in their units on the regular, like chicken sandwiches, frozen pizzas, hot wings, etc. The inmates can't touch the money, so if they want some food out of the vending machine, they can only walk so far and point to what they want. They can't go get it themselves. None of that.

However, the process to even reach the visitation room is the traumatic part. As a visitor, you get there and immediately fill out all this paperwork. Then you get searched as if you're a criminal, so your privacy's almost getting violated off the gate. This is every time.

There's a dress code for visitors, and we've seen people who have traveled several hours to come and see a loved one but can't get in because a visitor is out of dress code. It can be something as simple as the color you have on. The inmates wear a khaki outfit, so you can't wear khaki because that's what they wear, so it blends in. Somebody might come with khaki pants, not realizing they're violating dress code, and can't get in. Your best bet is to try to find a local Walmart or Dollar General to buy some raggedy clothes just to meet dress code.

However, keep in mind that you are trying to impress your loved one as well. You want them to see you looking nice for the short amount of time that they do get to see you. When you're a child visiting, you want to show your dad some stuff you've got, so you might put on an outfit that you think looks good to impress him. Again, I'm still that child that's looking for approval. Or y'all may have photos scheduled and no one wants to look crazy for the photos.

If you're not up to dress code, you quickly have to decide if you have enough time to buy some different clothes. That's happened to us before. My cousin had to sit in the car and miss a visit because dress code wasn't met. It's up to the prison's discretion. They can change the rules. The whole time going up there, you're almost panicking because you don't know if you going to be able to get in or not.

We would always get there early in the morning when the inmates were doing shift changes. It is a normal day for them, so you're seeing the inmates walking, going where they have to go. There's a time frame on when you can visit, so we would have to leave home in the middle of the night. If cut-off time is 9:15 in the morning and you get there at 8:45, you're scrambling because it's going to take you 15 minutes just to get processed.

After you get searched, they stamp your hand, basically labeling you, because you have to show that you've been authorized to come in. Then you're going into the actual prison, through the prison doors, to reach the visitation areas on campus. Behind you, you're hearing those big deadbolt locks and horns going off to signal for a door to be activated. At the check-in desk, you show that you've been stamped. Once you're told where you're going to sit, you go sit down and wait for whoever you're visiting. You can see multiple families waiting too.

The inmates are escorted from their unit buildings to the visitation room to greet their loved ones. If timed right, you will see some walking to the visitation room while you are also being escorted in from the visitor area. Before the inmates reach the visitation area, they are strip-searched in a private room. At some facilities I've visited, my people would still be in handcuffs when they come into the visitation room. They remain in handcuffs until they're authorized to be seated. Then you're seeing your loved ones getting uncuffed, and when it's time to leave, they get cuffed back up. It's just… it's a lot. That's a lot to see. As a child, you know that your parent has done something wrong, but it's hard to process it as a kid just because you're not as knowledgeable about life. It's just very sad, very humiliating and embarrassing. And it makes you think. It puts you in that mind to wonder, how are they treated when nobody's watching? If this goes on and we can see it, how much goes on back here that people don't know about?

When the side door opens and an inmate comes in, it feels like a rush. It's a rush for the inmates too. Everybody's looking, because everybody's hoping it's the person that they are there to see. I mean, you've got a million types of personalities and characters behind prison walls. Everybody in there isn't serving time because they have physically hurt someone or have no regard for human life. You have people in for tax fraud, embezzlement, money laundering, gun charges, etc. The majority are drug cases, but you do have some that may have committed murder or aggravated robbery.

Then you've got the innocent-looking inmates. Like, what could he have done to be in here? You've got the guy who might be 80 years old coming out and you're wondering how long he's been serving. You have handicapped people coming out. You have the slightly abnormal-looking guy with his body covered in tattoos from head to toe. I'm telling you, that visitation room is different. Everybody in there is under the same time scrutiny, trying to get those minutes with whoever they're here to see.

My dad, he's an older version of me. Every time he comes out, he's got some kind of dance move. Every time! In front of the whole visitation room.

That moment never gets old. It's like a high, an intense adrenaline rush. You just get those butterflies. I always feel like that little boy when he's coming out, like if I wasn't so tall and so big, I would go run and jump in his arms.

When inmates know they're having a visit, they spend money to cut their hair, and to get their clothes ironed and starched. It's always a big day because a visit keeps them connected to the outside world and lets them know they aren't alone. In the pod where my dad stays now, he can see the parking lot, so he would always tell us, "I've been up since early this morning and I saw y'all pull up in that white truck. Whose car is that?" He wants to know everything!

My dad watched me play sports when I was 7 or 8. But I remember one time on a visitation when I was a teenager, I had to run something back to the car before we signed in, and I was thinking, "I wonder if he's looking right now." I just took off sprinting because I wanted to show him how fast I was. And now that I think about it as an adult, that's some corny shit. It meant so much to me for him to see that I was an athlete. Like, "I'm about to just take off running and see if he can see how fast I move."

I am the topic of his conversations a lot. Other inmates from his pod might come out and notice us, and ask him, "That's your boy right there?" He eats that up! He might turn to me and say, "I told ya boy, everybody in here know about you and them sports!" But the reality of it is, it's hard to sometimes tell how he's really feeling, and to really tune into him because everything is so playful, happy, joy, joy, gaga, with him.

I saw him break down one time when I was about 25 years old. Before one of our visits, my aunt had relayed some troubling information to him regarding someone in our family. As soon as he entered the visitation room, we could tell he was off and he couldn't hold it in. I mean, he lost it. Tears are pouring out and that's the first time I ever saw that. In prison, emotion is not common because it's viewed as weakness. His whole thing was, he felt helpless, because he was incarcerated. There was nothing he could really do about the situation.

He went down the line apologizing to all of us—me, my grandma, my niece, and my sister—just for not being there, leaving us, basically asking for forgiveness. He apologized to me for leaving me at such a young age, for me having to navigate through this world by myself and into a young man. To my granny, his mama, he let her know that it was nothing that she did, that these were solely decisions that he chose to make. His brother, her other son, was still in prison, so my dad was speaking for both of them and emphasizing how sorry he was. Same thing with my niece. When her father, my uncle, went to prison, my dad became a father figure to her. When my dad went into prison, he couldn't be the loving uncle she needed, and he apologized to her for that.

Then he got to my sister. My dad got locked up in April before she was born in October, so he's never had a free world experience with her. I remember him saying, "It is killing me to know that you're having to go through life experiences without your daddy." He was very, very emotional, and we were all in there crying. And man, that was a hard visit, but I think it was good for my sister to see that she has a dad that cares about her life. I had never seen my daddy in this state, and he is not a little dude. He is a built individual. To see him this wide open and vulnerable, I truly believe it strengthened our connection.

Visitation is eight hours, so you spend a decent amount of time sitting there talking. You open up so many wounds, so many emotions. Y'all laugh, cry, joke, you do the whole nine because you're trying to catch up on a lot of stuff. You're constantly looking at the clock because you don't want it to end. It's like time is speeding up, speeding up, speeding up. And then all of a sudden it's over.

When the guards say, "Fifteen more minutes," you start wrapping up but you're rushing through the things that you may have forgotten to talk about. Then the inmates line up at the door and get ready to be strip-searched again, and all the visitors get ready to go out of the other door. It's one of those things where you are literally looking behind you until you can't see them anymore. As you're being escorted out, you're still trying to have a conversation. Telling each other that you love each other, just whatever you can think of.

The way it's set up, when you're walking back to the main lobby, you can see the other inmates on the yard of the prison headed back to their cells. I would walk slow, hoping I could see my dad coming of out the door, just to get another look. We always do that. The security's trying to get you out, but we take our time to hopefully lay our eyes on him one more time. We know we aren't going to see him for a while. It's prison, so you never know what could happen. It could be the last time you see him at all. All of those emotions happen every time you visit. That's been the experience for over 20 years and counting.

I tell people all the time, I went to visitation rooms more than I went to church. Visitation rooms were a huge part of my childhood. My dad and my uncle grew up experiencing exactly what I experienced because their father served almost 20 years. He was locked up in Nashville. My granny took her boys to the visitation room every weekend. It almost seems as if psychologically it became a way of life for my dad and uncle. You become institutionalized if you go there too much. I've heard people say that they won't even take their kids under a certain age to visit their parents or loved ones. They don't want their kids to know that type of life exists. They don't want these kids to see that it's humans that get treated this way, and for the kids to think that this is normal. Because it's not. It's inhumane. Granted, there have been people who have done certain things, but man, life in prison is hard to see.

What made it harder was when I started seeing my brother go into that system after the accident. Because I know what these places consist of. I've been going to them since I was a baby, and I also know his character. He does not fit that environment. So, when I picture him convicted of something serious and potentially going into that environment, it weighed on me.

Have you ever been to court and watched somebody getting transported from jail into the courtroom? I can still see my brother coming out in his jumpsuit with an officer on each side of him, like he's a terrorist. His hands are shackled. His feet are shackled. He's trying to walk up to the podium. Those are permanent images that will never leave my mind. It's traumatic to the point where anything I see on TV regarding prison, regarding court, or anytime I hear sirens go off, my childhood experiences tend to sometimes play in my mind.

My visitations with my brother, like the early ones with my dad, were through a glass window. We never could touch him, so you're sitting in a cubicle and if you put your elbows out, you're touching both walls. You're very intimate. You have no choice but to look eye to eye. That in itself is not an easy task. You know how it is when there's tension, or just a lot of things going on between two people. It's hard to look eye to eye. You're looking all over the place while you're talking. And because you can't touch, you do things like put your hand up on the glass, as if you're high-fiving or fist-pounding. But obviously I can't feel him. He can't feel me.

In my family, it's not just my uncle, my brother and my dad. My favorite older cousin growing up spent time in prison. That's my granny's nephew on my mama's side. He was grown and I was a young boy, but he was just a cousin I always liked being around. I spent a lot of time around him, and he was our neighbor too. I used to go visit him when his mother would ride to West Tennessee to see him in prison. When he had a parole hearing, he had to sit in front of the board to see if they were going to grant him parole to be released, and I was there to watch.

Everyone in my family knows about these types of environments because we have people in there. Our dads, uncles, cousins and brothers. That's why it makes it that much harder when you go visit, because you already know what's going on inside those walls. You try to get every last look that you can, and by the grace of God, thankfully nothing terrible has ever happened. Where my dad is serving time is not that violent, but there are many other institutions where it is. All it takes is for the right person to make it violent. People get locked up every day. You don't know what kind of maniac might be there tomorrow.

We forget about our prison population a lot and we don't always understand that there are real humans in these environments. Yes, they're in there because they've done something incorrect. But we all have. That doesn't make them less of a person. They've done something they're paying consequences for, but they still should be treated humanely. Especially during the time of COVID, we know it's not adequate treatment in there. We know they don't give a damn. If Dad got hit with it, I mean...people were dying in there of COVID.

When I went to visit him during COVID, we couldn't touch and we had to stay six feet apart. Even before COVID, there was no privacy, so here you are trying to have intimate time with your loved one, catch them up on whatever's going on in your life, and you've got guards right here on either side of you. So, imagine trying to have a conversation. You're not going to scream. They're already in your business. And now the visit is only an hour. When you get up, you can't hug each other. Can't even give each other a fist pound. We just got to go our separate ways.

One time I drove three and a half hours to see him for one hour. Then I turned around to drive back home. For a moment I didn't like going up there and it wasn't because I was angry at him. It's just that the whole experience puts you in an emotional discombobulation, but I understood that response wasn't necessarily fair to him because of how much visitations mean to him. When I let my dad know that I was coming, he told me, "Man, it ain't even worth it." I needed to lay my eyes on him. I said, "Don't even worry about that. I'm going to be there."

I'm intrigued by prisons because they have always been a part of my life. Even now, I get on YouTube and watch prison documentaries like Lockup: Raw. I have always wanted to see what life is like in there. What are they going through? As a senior in high school, I toured the women's prison in Nashville and the Wilson County Jail in Lebanon. That early interest probably explains why I studied criminal justice in college.

I started out with a Health and Human Performance major because that's what my brother studied at UT Chattanooga. He said he was going to do sports medicine or something, so I thought maybe I would be a physical therapist. My grades were mediocre because I just wasn't into the class. Then I changed my major to business. That shit was boring! So, the more and more I thought about it, I realized that I was always infatuated with the prisons. I mean, I've been coming to these places since a baby. My classmates were always saying, "Dang, you know a lot about this stuff." I mean, I had years in the game.

As a college sophomore, I was really looking at my options and thought I could potentially be a lawyer one day. That's what made me start studying pre-law. I enjoyed those classes and the mental stimulation. I've always been curious about tapping into the unknown. Nobody knows what goes on behind the bars. Nobody knows. Nobody really truly cares. Once you get into that system for committing a crime, people pretty much wash their hands of you.

I wanted to learn, how does this process even work, from both sides? From the convicted person's part, what led you to do what you did? How did you get to this point where you've done something that's going to cost you time in your life? Also from the prosecution side, what decisions or determining factors are in place to decide how long and where this person goes for the rest of their life? I wanted to know about the core system itself.

I've always been a psychological individual. I love learning about the conditioning of the mind. I'm all about deep thinking beneath the surface, considering we are people of habits and learned behaviors. You don't just wake up and grab a gun and shoot somebody. Something has gotten you mentally to this point, whether it was self-inflicted or inflicted externally. When we toured these prisons, I would ask these questions to inmates because I try to get to know these people. Not by what you've done or what you are in here for, but who you are, for real.

There were so many women I talked to who were in there for killing their spouse. It's normally a domino effect. People get to certain places and do certain things because of something that has happened to them, or they've seen it growing up. Unfortunately, for a lot of these people behind these walls, a majority are born into dysfunctional situations. They have a disadvantage from the start with a target already on their back and never have had a voice to be able to explain it.

There are African Americans who grew up during the crack pandemic who were incarcerated back in the '80s or '90s and they are still incarcerated! It's always been absurd to me how a person can make a mistake, especially a non-violent one, and serve that much time. If you ain't killed somebody or had intent to harm, how can somebody lose so much of their life for doing something deemed as incorrect by law? I understand the law is a law, but it always interested me how you can really make one mistake and it can cost you an ample amount of time, and the people around you, for a very long time!

My granny drove us to Pollock, Louisiana, when I was 12 to go see my uncle in the United States Penitentiary. I was only 6 years old when he left, so we weren't close at the time. We were around each other, but I didn't have many memories with him. When my uncle saw that he was going to Louisiana, he thought, "Who do I know down there?" He told us about trying to find inmates from nearby areas of Nashville. And man, that place is every man for himself. If you ever get a chance, do your research on the prison in Pollock, Louisiana. It's one of the worst prisons in America. And here I am, 12 years old walking in there. Even though it took eleven and a half hours to get to Pollock, I wanted to go.

It's too dangerous to transport USP federal inmates over the highway, so after my uncle got his sentence, they flew him to Pollock in the middle of the night. These are long flights. Imagine your feet and hands shackled, sitting in a plane seat beside the other inmates. When they feed you on the plane, they do not take your shackles off. So, you still got to find a way to eat. He said they treat you like animals. There are multiple US Marshals with big guns in the aisle because anything could happen. They're transporting, quote unquote, "the worst of the worst."

In federal prisons, they separate inmates by level of prison. The low tier is a minimum security, then they have a medium, a max, and a supermax. My uncle was in maximum security for a non-violent crime, locked up with serial killers and vicious criminals. This is who he's doing his time with, for selling drugs. The crime rate inside the prison was absurd. When you do that much time inside that kind of institution, you get numb to seeing people being brutally harmed. That's just another day. You step over a puddle of blood and you just keep going. You might be on the bottom tier of the prison and see blood coming down the wall. Then you know something done happened upstairs. In the nature of that, you don't get in people's business.

My uncle was 26 years old when he received his two life sentences and was placed in such a violent institution for a non-violent crime. He himself was a high school and college basketball All-American. Now he's got to adapt to the environments of a jungle inside the prison walls. He's a fitness guru too. He works out real hard and that's what kept his mind strong. A lot of times, the weak get preyed upon. If they feel like they can get you, they'll take your food, whatever the case may be. It's survival of the fittest.

My uncle is a very intellectual guy. He followed his routine to the library every single day. That's where he spent his time. He don't do no hanging out. He ain't playing in basketball leagues. He don't do none of that. Mind you, he had two life sentences, so he's trying to work on his case. But just imagine thinking, "This is my reality for the rest of my life. And I'm 26."

He says that you can always tell when something's about to happen because you can feel the tension. Especially in the units, things get kind of quiet and it feels like slow motion. He said that every time that happens, the inmates who are out of their rooms start making their way to the wall. Even if people are playing cards or something, they start making their way to where their back is against the wall, to where they can see anything and everything that's getting ready to happen. Before you know it, you'll see somebody strike or take off running after a guy.

This story might be a little gruesome, but they were out on the yard one day and a fight broke out. My uncle said another guy got beat up really bad, so this particular incident was about retaliation. A dude was standing in a ducked-off area in the yard, like a little blind area, waiting on his victim to come through the door. As soon as the man came to the door, the other guy stabbed him right in the eye. All you see is a fountain of blood just shooting out. When things like that happen, the correctional officers come and shut the compound down. My uncle says it's like a crime scene. They'll tape it off. You find out if the guy made it or not if they bring the white bags out.

My uncle did over a decade in that particular institution before being sent to a medium security facility that was much more relaxed. He was granted clemency in 2016 and was released on August 12, 2020, after serving 20 years of his life. Like I said, I didn't really know my uncle well previously, but I can tell for sure that some of his ways now are institutionalized. For one, he's what some may consider a hoarder. Meaning he really won't throw anything away. He's going to try to hang on to anything and everything, because in there you got to make use of what you got. Let's just say he bought a little bottle of orange juice from the gas station. When he finishes that bottle, he will keep that bottle, refill it with sink water, and put the bottle back in the fridge. That would be his bottle of water. You can go get more, dude! You got cups! But things like that happen because you got to make use of what you got on the inside.

When he first came home, he wore the same clothes for probably about a week and some change.

He was getting up every morning, about 4 o'clock, and going outside to work out. He was in the driveway working with his back against the garage, to where he can see. He knew nobody could be behind him. I mean, that's nothing but prison. That was normal to him. It's almost like seeing a child grow up again. You know, not in a disrespectful way, but because they've got to relearn, or learn. The world is so different than what it was in 2000. That's 20 years of nothing but not knowing if you're going to make it to tomorrow, let alone being out in the free world.

One of the messages that I want to get across in this book is that those traumatic experiences that were humiliating and embarrassing really made me who I am today. The same things that hindered me as a child made me a successful man. Always wanting to be accepted or to have some sense of acknowledgment is what brings me that relentless grind to achieve. Because I felt like I wasn't getting recognition or acknowledged when I was young, it pushed me to go even harder. Now it's second nature to go hard. It instilled that foundation. Whatever it is, I'm going to make it happen.

With that being said, I still hated going to these prison rooms because of what I'm seeing. However, it changed my perspective and put me in tune with reality because now I understand that my life could be worse. I'd see 19-year-olds or 20-year-olds with 51 years of prison time ahead of them. I've seen a 26-year-old with two life sentences who hasn't killed one person.

Based on the generational cycles in my family, who was next to go to prison? Me!

Had it happened, the men in my family had already broken the ice of humiliation for me. It's one thing to be the oddball out. If everybody else did well but you end up being the one going to jail, that's one thing. But everybody else done went. So, if I go, this isn't unfamiliar to my family. That whole fear of letting people down was erased because everybody's already done it. What's the big deal about me doing it? I didn't really fear it. I'm not saying that's what I wanted to do, because I didn't want to go to jail, but I couldn't see my life past the age of 25 for a long time. Not to say I would be dead, but I'm saying I had no idea what I would be doing. I had never seen anybody do something that made me think, "That's what I want to do."

Even though I broke the cycle, it is a constant battle to overcome generational cycles. It requires extreme focus and discipline because life can change in the snap of a finger. I could be out having a night of fun and something silly happens, and that could land me in jail. I don't necessarily have to go out and intentionally do something to end up incarcerated. That's why I have to be aware of what I'm doing and how I'm moving. I understand that the trajectory of your life can change that quick. No matter how much money a person's got, no matter who you may think you are, there are certain things that you can't get out of. Some you can, but some you can't.

One thing to understand is that regardless of what your intent may be, how it looks or how a person sees it is what it is. What I mean by that is, the way that you carry yourself, the way that you present yourself, and things that you desire are going to be a direct reflection of how people view you. Perspective is key. Whenever I do decide to have a family, there are things that have to be instilled, especially if I have a boy. As a black man, there are principles he will need to be aware of while trying to be a black man in America.

As a black man, you need to know there will be things that your white friends can do or say and get away with, but it's going to be perceived differently if you attempt the same thing. I'm not saying you walk around with hatred or ill will, but you will need to be aware of that. There may be certain places you go, or certain rooms you sit in, where your voice may not be as valued. Your opinion may not hold as much weight depending on your presentation, your character, or simply your look. You need to be aware. Don't take it personally due to someone else's ignorance. Just be aware and move accordingly.

Now if people are trying to do business with you, you've got more leverage. But if I'm coming to work for you, or trying to get a job in your corporation,

I've got to fit in whether I agree with your perspective or not. Or else I have to go find something else to do. I'm trying to create that understanding in the next generation of men. Helping them understand it's very possible for you to have a different encounter when getting pulled over versus your white friend's experience. If you do get pulled over, try your best to comply with what's being asked. Whether you agree or not is beside the point. Every battle is not worth being won at any given time.

Do what is needed to neutralize the situation and then we take it into legal matters if you have been discriminated against. It doesn't make you less of an individual to do what you've got to do to get out of this situation and carry on. As long as it's not detrimental or harmful to you or a loved one, carry on. I'm the same way with racial terms. There's not really too much a person can say that's going to get me out of my character. A lot of my friends can never understand that. Some people view that as being weak. No. I just have emotional intelligence.

If somebody calls me the N word, chances are I'm going to act like I didn't hear you. But if I'm sitting across from a person who says it, I'm not getting irate. Now, I may say something, but I would probably handle it in a more diplomatic way. Maybe let you know how ignorant you are, or how ignorant you may sound, by what you're choosing to say to me.

But, again, it's about being aware that I have no control over the hatred that you have for me right now. I'm not going to try to meet that fire with fire. I'm trying to get people to create an understanding that we live in a world with a lot of things that are going to happen that are out of our control. It's on you how you react. When you let these things get you out of control, you give them the power.

I've seen my dad exercise these same things when the correctional officers abuse their authority. He's been locked up 16 years and his workout routine has been the same. A new correctional officer came in and said that my dad can't work out inside the unit. The exact same workout he has been doing this for years! Now it's a violation. So, my dad basically said, "You got it." He stopped his workout and got in the shower. Had he said something smart, that's a writeup. They can send you to the hole. He told me that he's too close to his release to be doing that.

In situations like this, you have to exercise emotional intelligence. My dad said he thought to himself, "I'll just find me somewhere else to do my workout when I can, and go on about my day." That attitude right there will get people through a lot of difficult situations that they encounter. So many different people get worked up and that response will create a whole other situation out of a situation that could have been avoided.

When I was visiting my dad one time during COVID, I could see that the masks they give the inmates are ridiculously huge. They slide off their face. We were in conversation, not really paying too much attention to the mask, but it slid off his mouth. The correctional officer stopped our conversation. He said, "Butler, if I have to tell you pull your mask up again, I'm ending your visit." He's talking up on the podium so everybody can hear it. My dad was like, "My bad, my bad," and just pulled it up. A moment like that easily could have sent him the wrong way.

The visitation room is just a place of zero respect. It's strictly a dictatorship. And you can't really challenge it because at the end of the day they can call off your visit whenever. They can kill it. Visitation over. You have no control. None. From a visitor standpoint or an inmate standpoint.

In the visitation room, you see a mixture of things going on. You have couples who are clearly arguing. You don't know what they're arguing about but the woman's not happy and the man's trying to explain his point. Or he's just sitting there because at this point the majority of the inmates are emotionally unavailable after they experience so much stuff on their own. She's sitting there crying and upset and he's got a stale look on his face. I've seen visitations end because there's a disagreement. The visitor gets up and leaves out of frustration. Gone. And the inmate just gets ready to go on back.

Then you see the family over here where it's a bunch of little kids, all of them trying to jump in their daddy's arms. He's trying to hold all of them at once while he's talking and everybody's loving that. You got young kids running around because they can't sit still forever. They're mingling with other kids, and the dad might go into the playroom because he doesn't get to spend much time with them otherwise. But again, the inmate can only go in certain places. There are lines on the floor that they cannot pass. They can't go to the bathroom in the visitation room. They've got to go to the one that's back where they came from.

Sometimes you see couples who are lovey-dovey. They can't stop kissing until the whole visitation's over because they ain't seen each other in a while. You might see the inmate whose parents or grandparents are visiting, and they're 90 years old and trying to stay in touch with their baby. He might be all they have. Or you see the young inmate who looks like he's 18. Just got in here and his parents are looking at their baby. There's so much going on, and all y'all in there with each other. It's a sight to see.

On the way back home from those visitations, our family would spend a lot of time reliving what we just did. Sharing the experiences, talking about, "Man, what about what he said? Did you see him do that?" Summarizing what just happened. You can tell everybody's in good spirits just from being able to see him. Even though it is sad, you try to think about all the positives. All the good times you have with them. You share the funny moments.

Even from the parking lot of the prison, you can still see into the courtyard. Until we pull out, I'm looking, trying to see. And I think I see him. I'm too far away, but I always think that's him.

8

TUNNEL VISION

The coaching staff from UT Chattanooga came to my home for a visit on that Tuesday after I packed everything up and shipped out of UT Martin. Because it also Christmas break, I had a little time to clear my mind and reset. They took my mom and me to a local steakhouse to sit down and discuss potential opportunities. Due to NCAA rules, I would need to sit out a year, but I still believed that I could get that year back as a fifth-year senior. Because I played only seven games in my last semester at UT Martin, rather than a full season, I thought that would cover the first half of my ineligible period. Then, I'd wait out the other half as a red shirt during my first semester at Chattanooga. I could practice with them through the winter and spring, and then when the summer rolled around, it's nothing but green grass ahead.

Coach Wade explained that he couldn't grant me a scholarship in the middle of the season, and then he informed us that I would need to pay for the spring semester. I would have to take out a small loan to cover pretty much everything. Financial aid gave me a little bit, but I had to cover everything outside of that for classes, books, and food. He promised he would do his best to make sure that I could get a job to help cut some of that cost down.

Chattanooga played MTSU that Friday, so my mom and I attended the game in Murfreesboro. By this point, I had already committed to Coach Wade. Tyler drove to the game separately from the bus, and I rode back to Chattanooga with him. The next morning, the team had film session, and I got introduced. Because I couldn't get housing, Tyler moved from the dorms into a one-bedroom apartment off campus, and I slept on an air mattress in his living room for the entire spring semester. Mind you, I'm here to play ball, but I couldn't play ball yet. But this also made my transition into Chattanooga easier because it kept the confusion down, instead of people thinking Coach Wade had been recruiting me all along. Basically, I was a walk-on. I enrolled as a student and just joined the team.

Every morning I'd have a workout from 5 a.m. to about 6:15 a.m., then go to breakfast and get cleaned up. On Tuesdays and Thursdays, I had class at 8 a.m., and on Mondays, Wednesdays, and Fridays, I'd start at 9 a.m. After getting some lunch, I'd be ready for practice by about 1:30 every day, unless it was game day. When the team would leave, I had to stay back because I couldn't travel with them. On practice days, we'd be done around 3:30 p.m. or 4 p.m. On the days I didn't work, I had study hall at 6 p.m. Otherwise I'd be at work.

The coaches had a relationship with Enterprise Rent-A-Car and they ended up getting me a job there as a service tech. Their airport location had its own car wash and vacuum station down the street, so I would get the cars from the return area, get them cleaned up, and drive them back to the airport. I did that from 6 p.m. to 10 p.m. on Sundays, Tuesdays, and Thursdays. Man, how fast the tables turn. I go from full scholarship to sleeping on my friend's air mattress within the span of two weeks. A huge transition.

That season, the team won more than 20 games but we were shocked to lose the first game of the conference tournament, which immediately ended our season. Coach Wade was pissed. Partly as a punishment and partly to get us ready for the next year, we started our workouts immediately after the season was over. Then, around March, rumors started swirling that Coach Wade may be leaving for Virginia Commonwealth University. We knew that he wasn't going to coach at the mid-major level forever. He's a high-major guy. And VCU is where he came from, so that was a heck of an opportunity, to go back to where you started as the head coach.

Finally, that spring, he announced that it was concrete that he would be leaving. So, here I am. Ineligible. Working a job at night. Paying for school. Living with my friend and sleeping on an air mattress. And the coach I came to play for, who was supposed to be getting me clear and eligible, is taking another job. At this point the season is over. There is no return. This was a very, very difficult period for me. I'm wanting to play on a team that's established, with a good culture, and now I'm going to have to prove myself all over again to a new coach. Remember, I just went through this transition at Martin. That's why I left. But at this point I'm confined. I could leave for a lower-division school, but that wasn't me. I wasn't built like that.

We didn't know who our coach was going to be for about two or three weeks. I'm just working out to be working out. I'm still not on scholarship and I don't know if I have the money to stay. I'm realizing that this new coach has the authority to come in and decide to not put me on scholarship. It's his call whether he wants to recruit some new guys. Granted, we were returning most of our players, so it wouldn't have made sense for him to do that. Coach Wade did say in his exit meeting, "Don't worry about the scholarship. I'm still going to take care of you." In my mind, I'm thinking, "How the hell are you going to do that? You're at a whole other school!"

That spring, our athletic director informed us that we were getting the assistant coach from the University of Florida, a young guy named Matt McCall. This was his very first head coaching job and he really walked into a good situation. So, just like Coach Schroyer at UT Martin, every coach that takes a new position has an obligation or responsibility to try to protect the core of the team from leaving, because that's what's going through everybody's mind. At UT Martin, that was me. Coach Schroyer did everything he could to make sure I stayed. At Chattanooga, I wasn't one of those guys yet. Whether I left, stayed, or dropped out, it didn't matter.

In my meeting with Coach McCall, he said, "Tell me your situation. Tell me your story." I broke it down to him and told him exactly how I got to where I am. Afterwards, he said, "OK, give me some time to work on it, and let me see where our opportunities are."

When a new coach comes in, a lot of times they bring in their own staff. They might be open to rehiring somebody who is already there, but most of the time it doesn't work that way. When Coach McCall came in, he brought his strength and conditioning coach and a mostly young staff. They were player coaches, good guys. Most of them had been at the University of Florida previously, so they all knew each other. They knew how to manage. They knew what talent looked like. On the positive side, a new staff meant a clean slate for everybody. I had a chance to prove myself to somebody who hadn't seen any of us, except on film.

He also brought in a head assistant coach named Reggie Witherspoon and he's the guy that saved my college life, to some degree. Coach Spoon was in his 50s, older than our entire staff. A bald, black man with glasses. Tall and skinny. He had been around the basketball industry for a while as head coach at the University of Buffalo and as a coach on the USA Olympic teams. We hit it off immediately. I can't tell you what it was, but we just gravitated toward each other. I think it might have been my outgoing personality. He used to always tell me, "Man, you're going to be a preacher. It may not necessarily be in a church. It may not necessarily be in a religious way, but your voice carries power. I don't think you realize it, but people listen to what you say."

Meanwhile I'm facing the hurdles of trying to get eligible. I'm listening to him, but I don't really give a damn of what anyone's talking about at this point if it's not directly related to the game. I used to wonder, why does he say those things? Now that I look back on it, even though I'm the new kid, my voice did matter in the locker room. I was able to establish a leadership role fairly quickly. It goes back to the things Coach James was saying at UT Martin. That part of me never left. I would still get in the gym early and stay in the gym after workouts. I led by example and players could see that. I was a likable guy, personality-wise, and my room was always the hangout room for the players and friends on campus. I could always break the ice or loosen up any tension in the room. And I'm still that way.

At this point, our team had the most wins in the state of Tennessee. Coach Spoon would tell us, "One thing about achieving great things is that you create a target on your back. Every single day, even when you play the worst team in the league, y'all's name is circled on the schedule because you're one of the better teams in the state." He would remind us that it's one thing to do something great one time or win some games, but it takes discipline and mental toughness to sustain that. He'd say, "You guys, y'all are the target. Y'all are the team to beat. Teams are having extra practices when it's time to play y'all. Teams are making sure they get their full amount of rest when they play Chattanooga. It's the highlight of their season to beat you."

His words still impact me. Coach Spoon made us understand that every day you have to be prepared. On and off the court, you have to be doing the right things to ensure that you're ready to perform. Getting your rest, putting the right things in your body, going to class, doing the things to make sure you can perform. And that's a life lesson too. People may experience a little taste of success and get complacent. Feel like they've arrived or whatever the case may be. The truth of the matter is, anybody can do something one time. Anybody. But can you sustain it? Anybody can purchase a home. Can you do the things to keep it? Anybody can purchase a car. Can you do the things to make sure you got your money for the car note every month?

All through that summer, I'm going back and forth with the NCAA clearinghouse, sending in paperwork and trying to confirm my eligibility. I'm doing workouts with the team but I don't even know if I'll be playing when the season starts. That July, I tweaked my ankle again by stepping on somebody's foot and ended up on crutches for two or three weeks. It gave me flashbacks of the state tournament, because again I'm in a position of trying to prove myself. I'm fighting for a scholarship again and here I get hurt.

True to his word, Coach McCall granted me a scholarship that paid my tuition for my senior year. The next big step was getting eligible. Whether I'm paying or on scholarship, I wanted to play. In September, I was informed that the angle of what we were fighting for had changed. The NCAA ended up counting the games I played in my last semester at UT Martin as a half-season, and they wanted me to stay on the bench until after Christmas to complete a full year of ineligibility. Coach McCall disagreed with that ruling, and he told me, "You may have to sacrifice your junior year, but we're going to try to get you eligible for a full senior year." They only had a few weeks to figure out how to do it, since the season was about to start.

In October, during the preseason, we were getting ready to go scrimmage Eastern Kentucky in Knoxville. We'd just finished our walkthrough and we noticed the compliance guy walking toward the bus. His job is to keep the communication lines open between the team and the NCAA. He comes up to Coach and says to him, "The email just hit. Oldham is eligible." When he said that, anyone for miles could have heard our team roar! Coach just yelled out, "HEYYY!!!" He used to be notorious for that. Any time we'd win a game, he'd walk in the locker room and just bust out! "HEYYY!!!" He did that every time, never failed.

Hearing that decision brought a huge sigh of relief. Meanwhile, my adrenaline is going crazy because now I could play in the scrimmage. And when I got a dunk in that game, I pulled up on the rim and kind of taunted the other team. Coach and the players understood my excitement. It wasn't even about the dunk. It was just the simple fact that today has just been a hell of a day. Finally, I can get on the court. I knew that I was going to get to play this year.

Our team was destined to do big things. We were even picked to win the conference in the preseason. However, my season started off slow because I'm still fighting for minutes. I was taking it personally but, man, we had a good damn team. As a coach, it can be hard to balance the minutes when you got nine or ten guys that can play. Everybody wants to play all the minutes, but the reality of it is, it doesn't work that way. I was still getting accustomed to playing in a new environment, a new gym, new teammates. Granted, I had been practicing with them, but competing in a game was different.

We faced the University of Georgia in our season opener and that game was packed. Georgia has a nice-size arena, but I could still hear my mom sitting way up top somewhere, screaming. I could pick her out. Out of thousands of people in the crowd, I knew exactly where she was. I did play against Georgia but not a whole bunch. I think I had five points or something. I wasn't getting heavy minutes in the first half of the season. I was on a "one mistake, you're getting pulled out" type of rotation.

I grew frustrated because I had been through so much to get to this point, and it's like, it still ain't working out! Another thing frustrating me about not getting these minutes was that my mom traveled to these games and I'm not even getting in. But never once did she waver. She used to always say, "Keep going." She wasn't like, "Put my baby in the game!" It was never that. She would just tell me, "Keep staying focused and keep working. Your time will come."

In my mind, my chances to play professional basketball after college were getting smaller and smaller, game by game. All I had left were these 20 or 30 games in my senior year to prove myself. It felt the same as my last semester at UT Martin, watching the game from the bench. And just like at UT Martin, we were winning, so I couldn't do too much griping.

By now, in roughly a year's span, I'd had four coaches. They're all different too. But you know what? I could take a piece of each one and apply it to me and mold it. They all gave me a certain type of mindset.

So, you got Coach James, who recruited me to UT Martin. A pure, genuine guy. Unfortunately we didn't win many games, but he was a great person, character-wise. He knew how to treat people. He knew how to carry himself as an individual, as a man. He's what you call a transformational leader. With him, it's bigger than basketball.

You got Coach Schroyer, who was extremely transactional, black and white about his business. But you need to have a little bit of that in you too. Basketball is a business. When you're on the court, you can't let your personal feelings get involved.

You got Coach Wade, who was a "What have you done for me lately?" kind of guy. If you score 30 points today, you are his guy. If you come out tomorrow and score two, he will literally tell you, "I don't know why I recruited you." However, off the court, he gave us the best care anyone could ever receive from a coach, as far as gear, accommodations, and the way we traveled. We had catered food almost every day after practice, but he worked the shit out of us.

And then you got Coach McCall. He let you be you. He wasn't a control freak. He was a young guy. He understood. Plus, he was a player's coach, so he instilled a lot of confidence in his guys. He gave us a lot of freedom, almost to the point to where we didn't trust him early on, because it was too free. We came from a militant coach who drills you, drills you, drills you, drills you, that works you into the ground. And then we get this guy, whose workouts are nowhere near as intense. They're not as long. They're simplified. We're just like, "Hold on, man. Something ain't right." It took a while for us to even trust what he was doing.

I think my best coach ever was Coach Wade. The dude is a genius about the game of basketball. He lives, eats and sleeps it. He's still that way. If you look at his basketball résumé, he's on track to be one of the better coaches the game has seen. By any means, he's going to get that competitive advantage. He grinds though. He won't cut corners. He just does whatever he thinks is necessary to get that competitive edge.

Coach Wade wanted us to show him what we could do in practice, in order for him to put us in the game. He had to trust us to be on this court. He would say, "It's not about you telling me, 'Coach, put me in the game so I can show you what I can do.' It's more about, 'Show me what you can do so I can put you in the game.'"

When we played the University of Dayton, they were on a historic winning streak and hadn't lost in their home arena in some years. They have a notorious basketball program. Right before we got ready to go play at Dayton, one of our star players went down in practice with a broken ankle. We knew our boy was going to be out for a while with this injury, possibly the remainder of the season. I'm thinking I'm about to start getting some minutes. I mean, somebody had to fill in, but unfortunately it didn't really work that way.

As the first man off the bench I get in the game and get a quick bucket. I'd been fouled too, and I made the free throw. I hadn't even been in probably 30 seconds and scored three points. I'm like, "OK, here we go!" Suddenly, Coach pulls me out of the game and puts the starters back in. I was just giving somebody a breather evidently. I think I played three minutes that game. We ended up winning, which was huge, and we're getting national attention because we're beating high-power schools as a little mid-major. So, now I'm really looking crazy if I complain. We're doing things the school has never done, and you're worried about your minutes? That's selfish.

At this point, my mind was made up. Fuck this, fuck this team, fuck basketball. I was just at wits' end, man. I was tired of having to constantly fight, fight, fight, and I'm not seeing results. And we're still in non-conference, probably four or five games away from actual conference time. We had another game coming up two days after Dayton and I'm in straight asshole mode. I decided that either Coach was going to kick me off this team, or he is going to suspend me. One of the two is going to happen today.

I'm standing on the sideline in practice with my arms folded. I'm not getting involved in practice when it was my time to get reps. First string runs a play, second string runs a play. I'm not even subbing in. You would have thought I was injured. I'm just looking. I ain't talking to nobody. Checked out completely. Coach McCall says, "Oldham, you going to get in practice?" I just acted like he wasn't talking. I didn't respond.

At this point it's evident something is up. So, he sent over Coach Shannon, one of the other assistants. Coach Shannon had a very personable approach, and knew how to make light out of situations. Not necessarily everything was a joke, but he always had this slight little grin to him when talked. I'm telling him basically to leave me the fuck alone. I don't want to talk right now. I'm not getting in practice. Now leave me alone.

I carried out this whole attitude for the entire practice. Normally I'm staying after practice, getting shots, but that day, I was trying to be the first one to get to the locker room, get my stuff, and go on back to the dorms. Coach Spoon stopped me at the door, and he said, "Whether you want to or not, we're fixing to sit down and have this conversation." I'm struggling to get through him to get out of the gym, and I told him, "No, we're not."

Again, he said, "We're going to sit down and have this conversation." I can't tell you what it was that made me do it, but I ended up sitting down. We sat in that gym for three hours after practice. Me, Coach Spoon, and Eric Robertson, one of the other players on the team that he invited to sit down and talk with us. The moral to Coach Spoon's message was that I needed to stop thinking so far ahead about how many minutes I wanted to play and to focus on the minutes that I'm actually playing. If I do that, I'll gain more minutes. He went on to explain that if Coach gives me more minutes, that means I'm on the floor more. And if I'm on the floor more, that means I have more opportunities to score.

"You're not even able to conquer the current moment, because you're looking so far ahead," he said. "This team is good. We don't need you to score 30 points. Everybody can score! Do things that impact winning! If you're snagging every rebound, Coach McCall is going to have to play you. If you're guarding the other team's best player, he's going to have to play you. These are the things that are going to lead you to more minutes, which will in fact lead to more scoring opportunities because you are on the floor more."

Coach Spoon told me that rather than focusing on thoughts like, "Well, he's about to take me out anyway," I needed to maximize the few minutes that Coach McCall gave me, so he would feel like he had to give me more. Then he told me, "Every day in practice, Coach McCall should have to tell you to slow down. Saying, 'Easy, we're just walking through.' That's how you get more minutes. All this pouting, and you're only hurting yourself. At the end of the day, if you decide to quit this team and leave, Coach McCall is still going to have a job. The season is still going to go on. The team is still going to be playing, and you're going to be at home."

I'm hearing all this, but at the same time, I'm still in my stubborn mode. I replayed this talk the entire night in my head and woke up with a different focus about me. The next day in practice, I'm just in a different mindset. I take heed to what Coach Spoon was saying. Even in the early drills that we're doing, I'm trying to destroy everybody. I'm doing what Coach Spoon said, thinking, "He's going to have to tell me to slow down because I'm going 100 from the gate."

Majority of the time, prior to my conversation with Coach Spoon, my mind was distracted when I would sub into the game. It's hard to play when you're in a mental funk. I wasn't shooting a great percentage at the time, so I started focusing on the defensive end. I'm guarding my man. I'm locking my man down, getting steals. I was probably one of the best rebounding guards we had. And I'm starting to notice, as time is going on, I'm getting more minutes. Minutes are starting to go from three minutes to 11 minutes, from 11 minutes to 15 minutes. Then I'm beginning to average about 20 minutes a game. When conference play rolls around, I'm getting more minutes and the team's still winning. It wasn't like I started playing more and suddenly we were losing. And man, what Coach Spoon said happened tenfold. I started focusing on the small things that created the bigger picture.

I never did become a starting player. I ended up being the sixth man with tremendous impact. Any time there was a close game, I would be in at the end of the game, because we needed a good free throw shooter on the floor. The last 12 out of 16 conference games, I think it was, I was averaging double digits, and I was top three in minutes on the team. I was coming off the bench, getting more minutes than some of our starters. My teammates respected that because I was grinding for it. I became a vocal leader on the team also. I was what some may consider the glue guy, and it sent a message to the other guys on the bench who felt how I felt, as far as they should be getting more minutes. Because I was able to stop getting so caught up within myself and started looking at the bigger picture, it seemed as if they followed suit.

Before you know it, we had a team environment and that's how we were successful. This is what made us such a good, connected team. People stopped caring about the individual accolades. If you got a guy going through the fire with you, and you see he's not giving up, you want to climb and keep fighting too. Had I been a jerk, pouting on the bench, upset in the locker room, talking trash about Coach, then that's called being a cancer, and that stuff trickles down. The other players who felt like I felt, never coming off the bench, would have acted the same way. The team would have been destroyed. That's how powerful it was. Because I went the other way, people followed that. I mean our team, we was tight.

Chattanooga is in the Southern Conference, which is a one-bid conference. That means only one team from that conference can go to the NCAA Tournament. At every round of the conference tournament, you win or go home. Any time that tournament play is a do-or-die situation, the game is completely different. What you've done in the regular season doesn't matter. There's a lot more pressure. Every shot counts because if you lose, it's over.

When we won the regular season championship, we advanced to the conference tournament in Asheville, North Carolina. First round, we played Samford University out of Birmingham, Alabama. We had taken them twice in the regular season, but they were playing well around this time. Close game, but we defeated them. Second round, at semifinals, we played Western Carolina. They snuck a win on us earlier in the season, but this time we beat them. Now, the showdown for all the marbles: Chattanooga versus East Tennessee State University. They're our rivals and they were a very, very good team. ETSU had a high-major coach and a lot of high-major transfers. We beat them twice during the season and we knew if we played them again, they were going to have it out for us.

By now I'm coming off the bench quick because the trust has been built. I'm playing well on both sides of the floor, I'm a vocal leader, and Coach McCall knows he needs me on the court. I'm playing almost the whole game. This visibility increases my chances to play professional basketball. I'm showing the fruits of my labor from continuing to fight, continuing to push. Sticking to the script is helping my dreams come true. I'm getting more recognition. As a team, we're playing on higher levels and winning games. We're steadily going further as a team. And in that conference championship battle, we defeated ETSU again and punched our ticket to the dance. The NCAA Tournament!

On Selection Sunday, we were matched up with the University of Indiana. We got a 12 seed, which is decent for a mid-major, and Indiana drew a 5 seed. A 12-5 game is one of the biggest upsets on March Madness brackets, because those teams are fairly even. It's a high-major most of the time, but it's not like a prestigious high-major that just can't be beat. Those 12-5, 11-6 and 10-7 games are your common upsets, where these low-major schools come in for the win.

The experience of qualifying for the NCAA Tournament is like nothing else. We are hyped! Your team takes a private charter flight and you're picked up at the airport. Getting off the bus, the hotel people are lined up and you can see the signs that say, "Welcome, Chattanooga!" Everything in the hotel is predicated to your university. It's almost like you're walking into a resort, a hella cool feeling. You get into your hotel room and your bed is laid out with March Madness gear, shirts, Chattanooga shirts, hats, backpacks, socks, shoes. I mean, just nice shit.

We played at the Wells Fargo Center in downtown Des Moines. We arrived on a Tuesday, but we didn't play Indiana until Thursday. In between we had open practice on Wednesday. Each team has a 30- or 40-minute slot to get accustomed to the court and get up shots. It's not really practice, but it's a chance for the fans in the gym to get autographs and to see their team. It's really for your big, high majors who have the stars.

I'll never forget, we're walking in the tunnel, just going to our locker room, and suddenly we see a bunch of people with cameras, guys pulling rope and a crew backpedaling, trying to make sure they're still in focus. Then we see John Calipari, the head coach at the University of Kentucky, walking through. This is normal life for him, but for us seeing that, it's like, "Dang!" This is a special moment! And then we see the whole team following behind him. I'm taking all of this in. At the end of the day, it's still basketball. You got to go out there and perform. But this type of attention and press wasn't common for our school.

My dad knew that we were in the conference tournament before I even called him. He watched the ticker on ESPN when the scores would come across, and he noticed UT Chattanooga when they would show the teams so far who were going to the tournament. When you punch your ticket, you get a small segment on ESPN and my dad saw that too. Over the phone, he told me, "I'm going to try to tell the correction officers to put this on the TV."

Never in my life, had my dad watched me play basketball. He'd only heard about it, and now his first time ever seeing me play was going to be on TV on the biggest stage ever! When we talked about it later, he said he couldn't sleep the night before. It was almost like he was about to be playing. He told the whole compound his son was going to be on TV, and at tip-off, chairs were lined up in the compound with everybody watching the game.

Right after I transferred, UT Martin played a TV game against Butler University. I hadn't talked to my dad in between time when the transfer decision had been made. So, when he saw that UT Martin was getting ready to play, he tuned in to the game, thinking that his son is going to be on there, and I wasn't. When we caught up on the phone, he was like, "Boy, you must've got in trouble with someone! Did you not travel with the team?" That's when I had told him I transferred. He said, "You got these people in here looking at me crazy!"

At 20 years old, I still had that sense of wanting to impress my father. The NCAA Tournament was my first chance to be able to do that, and really my only chance. Being a senior, and based on his prison time, there wouldn't be another time. I would be done with sports by the time he got out. Again, it goes back to the visitation room, and when I took off running because I wanted him to see how fast I could run. Knowing that he was watching the game was a special moment. I didn't share that with anybody because I didn't want to overwhelm the situation. I wanted to still stay locked in and play. I knew I had to perform.

Dre drove to Des Moines to catch that game. J-Dubb, my boy at UT Martin, came with a few more of our friends. Mom was there, obviously. On that stage, a lot of people play nervous because there are a lot of eyes in the arena. You're nationally televised. NBA scouts everywhere. It's just a lot going on if you're not used to that. It's a huge moment to soak in, but you don't have much time to soak it in.

I had a very good game, but we ended up losing. That was how my senior year ended as well as my college career. But I was at peace with it. I mean, I didn't want to lose, but I was at peace with how I played. I felt fulfilled because I played well. It was a stitch to that wound as a child of not being seen or acknowledged by your dad. Playing in the NCAA Tournament gave me a chance for that to happen. Honestly it helped me perform because I didn't feel self-conscious. I was just going out there like I was backyard hooping and it worked out in my favor. My dad got to see me perform well and not get out there and look like trash. That would've eaten me up.

After the tournament, I just remember sitting back and thinking, 'Damn, what if I would have had my junior year?" That's what I've always wondered. Would things have been different for me? I only got three years of college ball, and you're supposed to get four. I ask myself to this day sometimes, what could that extra year have done? What would my sports journey have been like if my father was around?

9

TOXIC SMILE

Between that gap of basketball being over in March and my college graduation in May, I started wondering, "What next?" I felt like everything could be coming to an end if I didn't have an opportunity to play professionally, which a very small percentage of college athletes do.

I see a lot of people, to this day, who prefer staying attached to a familiar area, where it feels comfortable and calm. They've been doing it all their lives, so they'll spend an extreme amount of time on something that might be just a hamster wheel. I've also seen guys who are well-established in their career, but they're still trying to get overseas, or still chasing the pro dream. It's a thin line between never giving up on your dreams and just re-channeling your energy and your focus. It's a thin line.

I still had the hunger to play, as I mentioned, so I kept working out in the off season as if I was preparing for another upcoming season. I continued weight training and skill work, just like I had been doing the previous years. Also, I started reaching out to agents for representation to play professionally. That same routine from high school, contacting coaches and trying to get a scholarship, kicked in again. I put résumés and highlight films together, going back to the structure of being an advocate for myself, hoping to get another chance.

I'm emailing numerous agencies and even sending things to teams overseas. The website for the International Basketball Federation, also known as FIBA, lists all the teams in every country. I obviously didn't have contact information for all of them, but I would browse the countries that I wouldn't mind going to and look at their teams. I always started with teams that had the worst records because I knew they would be in desperate need of players. Then I would find their coach's name or the team organization and get on Facebook or Google to try to figure out how to contact them.

I got some hits back, some interest. Then I landed an agent out of Australia who gave me a chance. He wasn't with a big-time firm but all I needed was an opportunity. He signed me early on, right around graduation, after he watched me play in the NCAA tournament. But he couldn't find a spot for me in time for the fall season. Most of those jobs start in September, then the spring leagues usually start in February or March.

I'm kind of going through an identity crisis at this time. I'm still chasing the dream to play overseas, but I don't have a job at the time. I graduated college with a degree in criminal justice and I moved back home. I understood that basketball's what I do. It's not who I am. But at that time, I hadn't done much else, so I didn't know what direction I wanted to go if I didn't play ball. Then again, I was fresh off a good season. I knew I could do it. I felt like I was capable. To me, it was more of a matter of time versus wondering, "Am I good enough?"

I didn't want to come back home only to get caught in that small-mind, small-city mentality, and just get me a job in corporate America clocking in and clocking out every day. There is absolutely nothing wrong with that, but it just did not fit my mentality, especially at this time. I knew I was capable of more, so I had to challenge myself. I had to get in uncomfortable areas. I knew that I wanted different scenery. So, I moved to Nashville with Grandma, my dad's mom, instead of back to Lebanon with my mom, and took on the world from there.

Granny doesn't generally express too much emotion. Just direct, straight to the point. Very, very honest. Very, very caring, though. She loves her family. It was good living with her. She has a nice house, and she don't mind cooking! As a kid, my visits to her house would be sporadic, every now and then on weekends. We've always had a good relationship. I just never spent that much time with her, all at once, so this felt new. It was just her living in the house, so I had a decent amount of my own space.

When I was still trying to get a contract, I was going to different basketball showcases too. Trying to get exposure at camps. My brother and I flew out to Las Vegas for an exposure showcase out there during NBA summer week, a big-time showcase. We had a good time out there. That was a good bonding moment for us to just be kicking it in Vegas.

However, this is when I almost veered off, during this time right after college. I picked up a job being a neighborhood HOA manager in Lebanon, Tennessee. I sat in the neighborhood clubhouse every day for around six hours. Easy job, but it was a different transition. The benefit of that job was that the clubhouse had a weight room. I would work out every morning before work, so it allowed me to stay fit. Then after work, I'd go play pickup basketball somewhere. That job was very, very flexible. It allowed me to still do what I needed to do.

Again, times were hard because everything with the sports side felt like slow motion. I'm trying to get overseas. Nothing's coming through. I'm seeing other guys getting contracts and leaving for their seasons. I'm still here in Nashville. So, through this trial and tribulation, I'm still in contact with the same friends I had growing up, except now I'm more accessible because I'm back home. This is my first time living at home since high school four years ago.

The clubhouse wasn't paying me well. I was getting $14 an hour, but only working five or six hours a day. That's not even $100 a day. I'm getting roughly $600 to $800 every two weeks. What is that doing for anybody? Before I knew it, I started slowly falling into the habits of the circles I was hanging around. I'll never forget when I called a friend who was heavily involved in illicit transactions. I told him, "I need to make some more money."

My whole thing was, I feel like I can do it. I feel like I can be good at it and stay under the radar. Nobody would ever expect me to be doing that. I'm the college kid who just graduated. I told myself, "I know at least be able to stay clean for enough months to earn some stacks of money. Then I'll stop." That's what everybody's going to say when they start: "Just a few times."

Sure enough, he directs me to the source. My friend gives me top-to-bottom instructions on what I needed to do, where I needed to get the drugs, and how much money I needed to bring back to him. Then the rest is profit. I ended up meeting with the man, what they call a plug, and I picked up my first pack of weed. The mission had been to not fall in that cycle, but I found myself slowly falling in that cycle.

Now that I consider myself a drug dealer, a drug dealer has got to have somewhere to keep his drugs. So, I'm living with grandma and storing it in her attic. She has no idea – and still doesn't. She's about to find out. Any time my cousins would come over, I always had the weed for us to smoke because I was the weed man. I always had the supply for us to smoke.

I didn't have a huge clientele. Even though I knew a lot of people, I didn't want all of them knowing I was doing it. But some of the clientele that I had were guys who somewhat looked up to me. It clicked quick for me when they would ask me, "What are you doing?" I remember one time, one of the guys asking me, "How long you been doing this? You're supposed to be the basketball superstar." When he said that, I told him, "I do a little bit here and there," without him not knowing I'm new. He's damn near my first sale.

Before long, I had my weed and I bought my first gun. There was no correlation to getting a gun and being a drug dealer. I was a firm believer that when I turned 21, I needed to carry a handgun for my own safety but the right way with a carrying license. It's not a toy. It's not something to be flashing around. It's not something to play with. So, for four to six weeks, I'm riding around every day with an ounce of marijuana and a pistol. The starter kit to throwing your life away.

When I went to go train with Dre, I told him, "Shit hard right now." I had the goods in the car while I was in there training with him, and I told him about it. We had a long conversation regarding my decision. He was like, "Man, you need to call that dude right back and take him his stuff back." That was the moral to what he was saying. "You need to take him that shit back right now." I was like, "I ain't doing that. When we get done training, I'm fixing to go get this money. I'm going to make this play." I was selling it and smoking it, but I've never been a heavy smoker. Never. Even then, I would smoke from time to time, but I've never been that kind of guy. I gave it up that fall, sometime in October. After Dre consistently drilling into my head how poor the decisions I was making were, I finally came to my senses and asked myself, "What are you doing?" I used to be paranoid, just riding around with it in the car. I never did get caught with it.

Then, in December, I finally got my call that there's a team in Australia that's highly interested. So, after going back and forth with the coach, we came to terms of agreement on the contract. I'd be playing in Adelaide. That call came at the perfect time because who knows where I'd be otherwise. Seriously. Again, the work ethic had already been instilled in me. Dre put a curriculum together for me to take to Australia, a workout that I needed to be doing on my own time. Outside of what the team orchestrated, he showed me the extra stuff I needed to be doing.

Dre and I were still training up until I left for Australia. Everything he was still telling me was still coming true. Stick to the script. Stick to the script. I could have thrown my life completely away. All it would have taken was one traffic stop, or one transaction gone wrong, anything. That's all it takes, wrong place at the wrong time. It might not have necessarily be my fault, but here I am with illicit goods on me, and that's how my story ends.

Same as my dad, that's how it ends. He was a college athlete. He graduated college. What's crazy is, when I've had conversations with him, he told me he didn't start dibbling and dabbling in the drugs until after he graduated college. He had a job, but the fast lane caught up with him. Exactly the direction it was heading for me.

I flew out to San Diego that December because I had a friend out there playing for the Chargers. We were celebrating New Year's Eve when my mom texted me and said, "Let me know when you get a minute. We need to talk." Whenever a message like that comes through, I believe it is natural for everybody to get a little worried. Especially considering that she and her boyfriend had just dropped me off at the airport that morning. I stepped outside of the hotel room and gave her a call. She had finally built up the courage to tell me she was getting married. She said her boyfriend asked her to marry him. It kind of threw me off, because I'm thinking "Why didn't y'all tell me when I was in the car?" That flight to San Diego was an early flight. He was driving. She was in the passenger seat. Nobody said anything about an engagement.

After I got off the phone, I'm trying to process the brief conversation that just took place. I'm like, "Wait a minute. Order me another shot please!" So, that's how I found out that my mother was getting married. She's never been married. This is a big moment. I didn't really know anything about the man she was marrying. I know I'm not her dad. I'm her son. But at the same time, for 45 years, it's just been Mama. So now I'm being presented with blending a family. That's not common in our household. That's not familiar to me or my brother. What does that even look like? It was really one of those things like, "This is the new reality."

My mom threw me a going-away party on February 11 with a very good turnout. She was nervous as all get out, sending me that far. People were so caught up in the fact that I was going to Australia, but in my mind, it was always the bigger picture. Yeah, I'm going to Australia, but I'm going for a purpose. I'm not going on vacation. I'm not going there to lay on the beach and feed kangaroos. I'm going there to handle business because I'm trying to go to the next level. I flew to Australia with a clear mind and a mission. Here's my chance. I knew going in that I would be focused.

At the waterfront condo where we stayed, I had access to a gym, a treadmill, and workout equipment. I lived with the other American on the team, a guy from Chicago named Harold. A lot of times, my teammates would ask me, "Are you enjoying the experience?" Because sometimes I wouldn't go out. I wouldn't be out partying. I wasn't out chasing women. There's a lot of accessibility over there, especially with you being American. You're something different. Women gravitate toward that, and the status of you being there as an athlete. I would indulge from time to time, but I never allowed it to become a priority or a distraction to why I was there.

I did go to Melbourne with one of my other friends, but even that was a business trip. We went to play in a showcase. Melbourne puts you in mind of New York a little bit. Even with that being said, as I look back on it, I may have missed out on some of the experience of Australia, but it worked out for the greater good. Like I said, there were times where my teammates were out kicking it, and I'm in bed because I'm waking up early to work out or practice some skill work.

I did this over the course of the entire time I was in Australia and it showed in my performances. Everything that came to light that people observed was a result of what was done in the dark. It took some extreme discipline because I do like to party. Don't get it wrong. I like to kick it. But I was trying to achieve something else. This was not the final stop for me. I still enjoyed it, but I could have been more of a loose cannon.

Before going to Australia, I might have done some homework on the internet, but I hadn't seen this team on film, and I really didn't care. My first impression was, "I'm about to take over this shit. Can't nobody here fuck with me." That was my mindset. It was an area of swagger, but at the same time, man, you almost have to have that when you're on an island by yourself. I'm 23 hours away by plane. I don't know a soul out here. Nobody. Nobody knows me either. Whether I succeed or don't succeed, these people don't care. They don't know me. You have to have that sense of self-belief to where it's like, "By any means." I'm going to make it happen. Whatever it took for me to go out there and dominate, to make my people proud back home, to earn another contract for the next season somewhere else, I was willing to do that.

My whole time in Australia, I'm having breakout games, 40-point games. These games were streamed so my family at home could watch it on the link. Mom even came to see me in Australia too. I'm glad she got to experience that with me. That was a very, very good time. We toured the city, went to feed the kangaroos, and went to a safari zoo where you get to go out with the animals. We went to go see penguins. Ate at some nice restaurants. We did a lot. I remember that feeling of my mom being able to experience that with me. It was a surreal moment after everything we've been through in our lives. To be in another country together, that's big. She didn't get to see a game, though. We didn't have a game that week.

Being an American, the sports supporters and boosters treated me a certain way. But nobody in the city really noticed me until when I started doing my thing. When I started balling and word was getting around, I knew of a few restaurants where I could go in and eat for free. One time I walked into a sub sandwich place and a guy hollered out, "MVP is here!" He put two subs in front of me, took a picture with me, and used it for advertising.

That kind of attention was new and it's kind of like a high. What people also need to realize is, that ain't real. It's approval but it's approval based on what you are doing for somebody. They loved me because I played for one of their favorite teams and was performing well. That same love wasn't for every American basketball player that was over there. You've got to be conscious of that. It's a high. Enjoy it. Embrace it. Don't get indulged in it, to think that it makes you superior, above, or that you've arrived. Because as fast as you received it, it can go the opposite way. Quick. It's a temporary feeling. The same thing that makes you laugh can make you cry.

The majority of my time over there, I experienced that level of attention. But at the same time, I'm getting the recognition on social media because my family back at home is seeing what I'm doing. When you consider the times we're in, especially with social media gratification, the focus for me was never, "I'm trying to be famous." Stick to the script. Keep your eye on the main thing and everything else will fall into place. It's like trying to be a tremendous chef. In order to be a good chef, you've got to focus on putting the proper ingredients together. Then the food is going to come out and be delicious. The right result will follow if the necessary steps are taken

That would be my message to the young generation: Do not get caught up in the hype. Stay grounded. I'm not going to say that approval doesn't carry any value, but it's not real in a lot of cases. It's not genuine. It's simply based on transactional support. Appreciate it but continue striving. Focusing on the day-to-day process is what gets you the result. The gratification is just a result. Money is just a result. The house is just a result. You've got to do the proper things every day to build your credit. You've got to get up and do the proper things every day to provide the service you provide. That's the philosophy to achieving. Embrace the process, not the result.

Around July of 2017, I earned another contract to play the following season in Doha, Qatar. They wanted me there on October 1. I knew that I would be going to be home sometime in August, depending on how we did in the playoffs. Then after Mom's wedding in September, I'd be shooting right back out to another country.

I had a few rough games in Australia, but for the majority, I pretty much balled the whole season. I had a coach who was basketball oriented. He was a student of the game. I stayed focused. There were some other good players in the league, for sure. Times had changed. When we played teams that were considered top teams in the league, I was at their neck.

At the semifinals, we faced a team called North Adelaide, a rival of ours. They were projected to go to the championship, but we beat them in a very close game. My roommate Harold was celebrating and wound up getting into an altercation at the end of the game with the other team and their coach. They suspended him from the championship game. As the other American, we done worked all this way to get here and now he couldn't play. It felt like being back in high school, where all the weight is on my shoulders again. I'm the only American on the team. We're going against the Southern Tigers, who had won the championship for the last two years.

That championship game was up and down, like we were trading baskets, but I created a gap in the game in the fourth quarter. I erupted. I think I came down and hit three threes in a row. That was a magical moment. I was getting MVP chances at the free throw line in the arena. I was just in my zone. The crowd was just going haywire because the team had never performed like that.

Thinking about the feeling now, I can't help but to smile. What I was experiencing was like an out-of-body experience. I worked hard to get here. Everything that I put in and everything I went through... This is why I did it. For this moment. I'm not saying that sports are the end-all be-all, but it was just a result of seeing your hard work pay off. That's always a beautiful feeling.

The first thing we did after winning, the whole team ran to Harold in the stands. We rallied around him because he was a part of it, even though he didn't get to play. That was a big moment for him. He's an American import and he's going back home. We're all taking pictures with fans, and things of that nature. That was a surreal feeling.

I went on to be all-league first team in Australia and a league MVP. We made history by winning that championship which they hadn't done in 21 years. There's a documentary that will forever be out, streaming in Australia, called 21 Years in the Making: Bearcats Rise to the Top. It's not very suspenseful, but it does have me on the packaging of the documentary. It just gives a lot of history of the team. Then it breaks down our championship run. For me, looking back, it's just the fact of knowing I left my mark in another country. That's the fulfilling part. Everything that happened there definitely fulfilled the purpose. That MVP recognition was a result of that curriculum from Dre that I was exercising, day in and day out.

So, we get to September and the wedding's here. That's really why I came back home for that short amount of time. I could have gone straight to the Middle East from Australia, but I knew my mom had a wedding. Big day. First time. I need to be there. I flew back home August 26, and I had to the end of September to catch up with family and embrace Mom's marriage.

My first week home, I went with my brother, three of my cousins, two friends, and a lady friend on a group trip to Miami, like a "welcome home" type deal. Kicked it there, had a blast. I was still training between time. This is my first time coming home with a little bit of money in my pocket. I feel like I had arrived. I didn't know how to act. I was viewed in a different perspective too. I was doing things that people in my area don't do. Not only have I been playing basketball on a high level, but I'm traveling and experiencing places that we only see in books growing up. You don't fathom being able to go to places like Australia. You see these things on Discovery Channel, but actually living there? That's not a vision in a child's mind where I come from. It's not. I wish it was more common.

Seeing my mom get married wasn't the easiest transition for me, because the whole time they were getting to know each other before marriage, I was out of the country. I didn't get to spend adequate time with her, seeing her in this light, or get to know him either. It was like, "Hey, this is my fiancé and he's going to be around." We didn't gradually hang out more and more. It just became a thing. I didn't have to deal with it as much because I didn't live in Tennessee. My brother, on the other hand, did. Same for my grandmother, my mom's mom. Their perception may be more in-depth than mine because they were here, front and center. And I would be getting ready to leave again as soon I came back, so I wasn't going to get no time.

At the rehearsal, I learned that my brother and I weren't even in the wedding. That was a deep, deep gut punch for me. I didn't understand it. We were just going to walk her in and sit down in the pews with everybody else. I was uneasy about that. We had to rent a tux just like the one the groom had, as if we were going to be groomsmen. I should have just put on a damn polo shirt and jeans. We were the most important men in her life, especially considering her father was passed at this time. That's all it's ever been, us three, and we're not even involved in her special day.

I spoke my mind about it after rehearsal. Some changes were made, and they put us in the wedding, but it still didn't seem genuine and authentic. Why do I have to say this in order for it to happen? That stuck with me for a while, as far as my perception of them as a couple. Also, my perception toward him a little bit. I couldn't quite stomach how that situation could be possible.

My mom blamed it on somebody else who she said planned the wedding. She said she didn't have nothing to do with that. I'm not buying that. She took the easy road out. That pissed me off even more because you're not even taking accountability for your own day. If you want something to go on this day, it's going on. It's your day. You voice that.

Those beginning stages made it hard for me to really accept their marriage. Again, I'm not her dad. Nothing has to be run by me. I just felt like there was a lack of respect for me and my brother. From both of them. It wasn't just her husband's fault. He was doing what he was allowed to do. My mom never took a stance to initiate a change or make it any different.

The unhealed wounds in me were triggered, along with the rebellious nature. When I feel entrapped or confined in these situations, my initial instinct is to rebel. What it looks like in that situation is, "I'm not fucking with y'all, period. I'm going the other direction." It was easy for me to have that mindset because I'm leaving the country in two weeks. I don't have to be around y'all.

I knew around this time that I needed to go see a professional counselor at some point, just to help me with processing life experiences and traumatic experiences that I've been through. I didn't think too in-depth about it, but I knew I had an emotional detachment. I didn't want to cut my mom off and never talk to her again. That's not what I wanted, but these feelings were because of things that were happening now or had previously happened in my childhood.

In my opinion, if you get to that point, you've got some deep hurt. I knew I needed to figure out, where does that come from? Anytime you can walk through life and be detached from human connection, there's a deeper root to that. We're talking about people who can walk through life and be cold-blooded murderers. There's a deeper root to your lack of empathy for human connection. Why are you so cold? Why is it so easy for you to just say, "To hell with the next person"? Where does that come from?

At this age especially, my emotional intelligence was low. I didn't know how to express these things. I didn't know how to communicate them. I didn't even know how to process them. I just knew what I felt, and I didn't really feel respected. It goes back to those childhood traumas of not feeling acknowledged. It was really that inner child screaming that wasn't healed. My only instinct is, again, rebel. That's what I know at that time. Rebel!!

This is my own mom, the only person I've ever had. I didn't feel acknowledged, didn't really feel respected. I have never felt like she put a man before us. She's never done that, but I felt like she's putting my brother and me in a situation without any sort of communication. She's forcing us into an obligation without free will, if that makes sense. She's asking us to blend a family with somebody that she has never really introduced us to. In my opinion, there was never a blend, if that makes sense. We don't even know what that looks like, or how that's supposed to go.

Granted, she didn't either. It's her first time to get married. But we could figure this out together! It's not as simple as saying now you're in a relationship, and you're inviting us over to dinner with his family, and everything will be fine. We went through these hard times while they were attempting to blend the family dynamics. There would be times where they might be cooking dinner and I just wasn't comfortable. I don't know y'all like that. This isn't somebody random. This is my new family. It's different than just going to a work partner's crib or something.

If they were having dinner and I didn't necessarily feel comfortable going, my mom would accuse me of not liking her husband, saying, "I don't know why you don't like him." It's not that I don't like him. I don't know him. Again, these are people who we are planning to involve in a very intimate part of my life. I already struggle with intimacy with people. She's asking me to be in vulnerable, intimate environments with people that I do not know. It's like we didn't even preheat the oven. We just turned that motherfucker on high Fahrenheit and put the pizza in it. That was a hard transition for me. Very, very hard.

Shortly after the wedding, I went to the Middle East by myself as a 22-year-old kid. I've been through a lot, so in my mind, outside of death, the worst things that can happen have already happened to me. I lost my dad at a young age. Not to the grave, but he was just out of my life. I done watched my whole family battle with prison and different kind of charges. Battle with failed relationships, battle with financial poverty. I done watched friends my age pass away, throw their life away, get sentenced to a lot of time in prison.

Seeing that type of stuff, what's left to be afraid of? The worst things that life has to offer I've experienced. Not necessarily firsthand, but on more than one occasion, I've seen dreams be shattered due to a temporary decision. I've seen lives be altered due to a night of fun. I've seen those nights change a person's entire trajectory of their life.

I've seen people go through the grind of college, put the work in, and graduate college, only to serve more than 20 years in prison. I've seen young guys my age get stuck in the place I was in when I left college, that identity crisis, who overdose on drugs. If they didn't overdose, they're currently functioning addicts. I've seen it.

Fear really just comes from the thought of the unknown. You're afraid because you just don't know what's on the other side. You don't know.

I tell you what's fear. Fear is sitting in the courtroom while your loved one is standing in front of the judge waiting for him to announce how much time they're fixing to spend in this prison. Fear is not knowing if there's going to be enough money for y'all to pay the rent, so y'all might be outside. That's fear. Ain't no fear about trying to perform a basketball task and hear a team just say you're not good enough. OK, if they do say you're not good enough, what's the worst that could happen? What are you scared of?

Fear is getting that phone call at 5:00 in the morning that your brother was just in a deadly car accident. That's fear. Fear is calling your dad's phone numerous days in a row and getting no answer or response. That's fear.

Once you've experienced that, it's almost like your fear meter is empty. You done wasted all your fear. All your fear has been used on life events. I don't have much fear in me to experience. What I once feared and was embarrassed to discuss, that's what made me who I am. Those stories are why I'm able to relentlessly push and pursue my goals. I'm fearless. I am completely fearless.

I don't view it as failure if something doesn't work out. People are always thinking, "If it doesn't work out the exact way that we planned for it to work out, then it failed." But who's to say that your plan was the best way for it to go? There are a hundred ways it can happen. It doesn't mean it's not going to happen.

On my way to Qatar to play basketball, my mama took me to the airport. She was a little bit upset because I was going to the Middle East, just not knowing much about it. It was kind of like an awkward dismissal. I was ready to get out.

10

RESPECT THE GAME

My transition to Australia had been easy. There's an accent but no language barrier. The food's pretty much the same. It's really like a mixture of Miami and California combined. That's how I would explain Australia to somebody that's never been.

The Middle East? Polar opposite. Culture shock. It's the Islamic culture. They speak Arabic. So, I'm now in a situation where I've got to figure it out. I felt myself maturing at a rapid pace. When you're overseas, you have a lot of time to practice stillness. You have a lot of "you time." This is when I started tapping into my thoughts and behaviors. I'm still reprocessing everything that just transpired this last month, dealing with my mom's wedding, but I'm doing it by myself.

Growing up in America, the only perspective I ever had about Muslims were radical Muslims and the 9/11 conspiracies. I was a little terrified because I'm thinking I'm going to be in the middle of a war zone every night, with bombs flying around. These are my mom's thoughts too. For the first two months, I was telling my mama that I'm coming home. Here I am, upset with my mama, but when things got hard, who do I run to? I'm still mama's baby at the end of the day.

Just before my contract ended in Australia, my agent and I terminated our agreement because I knew he didn't have the willpower to get me where I wanted to go. He got me in the door with Australia, but that was pretty much his ceiling. Then I signed with a big-time agency called Octagon Basketball.

One of my college teammates was playing in a league in Russia at the time and that's how I got connected with my agent Dmitry at Octagon.

I knew going into it that Qatar wasn't the best league, competition-wise, but it was good money. Going over there, the average pay is $5,000 to $10,000 a month with the opportunity to make bonuses if you advance in the playoffs. You get a check at the end of every month going to your account, and when you come back home, it's tax-free money. As a 23-year-old kid? Oh, hell yeah! And I'm playing ball to do it. A contract is typically for seven to ten months. They give you a car and a place to live, but you're paying for your food and what you do in your social time. When I knew the type of money that you can make over there, I said, "Yeah, that's a no-brainer." I did a good job saving while I was there. I looked at it as a job and tried to run the coins up as much as I could.

Doha, Qatar, is directly across the Persian Gulf from Dubai. A very, very, very rich area. They have an airport called Hamad International, which is one of the most luxurious airports in the world. They drive G-Wagons, Ferraris and McLarens around like we drive Toyota Corollas. That's their vehicle to go to work every day. They don't really place significant value in those things like we do here in America. Money's just different there. I mean, they're aware that these are nice cars but it's just different.

In Qatar, the hierarchy makes the decisions of what goes for the masses and that's all the way from government to places of employment. It is a dictatorship. Women are not considered equal there. They have a role that they play, from employment to relationships. They cover themselves and practice their religion very heavily. Every few hours, you would hear the call to prayer throughout the city on intercoms. The locals would stop whatever they were doing and pray. My teammates would step out of practice for a moment, and they would all get in their formation on the side of the court and do their prayer.

There are also a lot of Africans from Senegal that have migrated to live in Qatar. You have others who are from Egypt and that area. There are a lot of European women who come to Qatar after enrolling in a popular flight attendant program with Qatar Airways. Meanwhile, I had teammates from Jordan and Lebanon, and even one from Harlem, New York. In other words, there's a plethora of foreigners coming through there on the regular. I'm meeting people from the Netherlands, from Greece, from Bulgaria. I mean, everywhere! These people are out in the clubs, out at the bars, out at the social areas.

The city itself is gorgeous. I didn't get my car from the team until around my second month of being there, and the street signs are in Arabic, so I'm walking to a lot of places trying to figure out what's going on. Qatar is the total opposite of what I thought it would be. They've got clubs, they've got nice restaurants. A lot of it's on the water, and you can ride four-wheelers in the sand, rent dune buggies, go to the beach, etc. People sit around outside of warehouses or shops sipping tea. Drinking tea together is a huge camaraderie deal. Going to get tea with somebody is real bonding time. Here we may say, "Hey, you want to meet up and get coffee or go have a drink?" Tea is their deal. Tea and hookah. You can go anywhere and get you some hookah.

There's also an Army base there, so I met a lot of U.S. military people. One of them happened to become a long-term lady friend of mine. I met Jess through my teammate who had been kicking it for a while with a girl he met on a dating app while we were there. When they made a date to go to Nobu, she wanted to bring one of her girlfriends along which happened to be Jess. So, she asked him if he had any teammates to make it a couple's night. When he told me this, I asked, "What does she look like?"

Really, at this time, I hadn't been in Qatar that long and didn't know if I wanted to get out in the city like that. I do like to get out and kick it, but I really didn't want to go. Then she sends a picture of Jess and that's all she wrote. I'm seeing that she looks nice. She was 30 years old, and you could tell that she was a grown woman. I'm like, "I got to be on it when I get there." I go in the closet and find a Burberry shirt, some black pants, some black Cole Haans and getting fresh as I can be. I'm a little intimidated, because we were meeting through a mutual friend, and that's pressure itself.

The two girls were already at the Sheraton hotel bar when we pulled up. I see her and it was everything the picture showed. I'm like, "Damn. This is real." Then we migrated over to Nobu, which was right next door. She ordered a double shot of Hennessey black. I'm trying to get her attention so I'm taking her bill and mine. Neither of us knew that it was a $150 drink!

The girls brought another friend in the military, so it was the three of them, my teammate and me. We just had drinks and enjoyed each other's company. We didn't even eat. That was the day I lied about my age because she had asked how old I was and I said, "How old do I look?" I put the ball back in her court. She started guessing I was 28, and I'm like, "You're right around the right age." I got away with that for a little while, actually for months. She would constantly bring it up later on that I lied about my real age on our initial meeting.

I started getting more comfortable in Qatar when I met Jess. She's from Atlanta, which is four hours from my home, so we shared a lot of similarities as we went through this unfamiliar territory together. That made it a lot easier, and it also made it more entertaining. We started exploring the city together. Outside of work, I had something look forward to, somebody to share my experiences with. Somebody to talk to, and to figure things out together. She had traveled a little more than I had because she had been in the military for 10 years, but she was having new experiences as well.

We spent our first date night with just us two at the DoubleTree Hotel, which had a nice restaurant downstairs and a rooftop bar. To be on a date and to have undivided attention with somebody else in an intimate way—that was all unfamiliar to me. You don't have friends or other people to distract you. It's me and you, so the level of engagement is just completely different. You better have some conversation about you!

One day, I took my shirt off at the beach and she asked me, "What the hell is that on your chest?" I didn't even think about it, but she saw the tattoo of my birth year: "Est. 1994." I still carried out the lie. I was like, "That was my baby brother's birth year, he passed away at birth, so I got a tatted on in his memory." Which was far from the truth! It was really childish, now that I think about it, but it was my fear of her not wanting to deal with me anymore. It was my fear of her not being interested. Instead, she just said, "You a baby."

Jess opened my eyes to more mature behavior, because truth be told I never spent much one-on-one, intimate time with women leading up to that.

High school, none of that. In college, it was strictly transactional. Y'all do what y'all do, then carry on. Outside of that, my teammates were around, so everything is more of a group environment. This was the first time I started experiencing true intimacy and quality time with someone that I really cared for.

We had fun, man. She was my friend. She was very attractive to me as well. Along with the other stuff, we just had a good time together. That's what I liked and that was really my first time having that type of interaction with a mature woman. There were no games involved. She was brutally honest about what her situation was. She had a 10-year-old son back at home from a long-term relationship that had led to a broken engagement, so she had a lot more real-life experiences than I had as a 23-year-old.

She helped me grow up, but at the same time, I knew that this could only go so far. That may have been what made it a little more enjoyable, because there was not much pressure to perform after a while based on our life situations. We were literally just two good friends kicking it. She was at a point in life where she already knew what she wanted, and what she was and wasn't going to put up with in a man. Didn't want any more children, etc. She'd been through all the youthful stuff that I was just now getting into.

There would be times where I would still maybe sabotage it a little bit, just because I didn't want to get too close. I'd think, "Man, I could be a stepdad at 24." I didn't think that would work, and there were still parts of her life that I didn't quite understand. Such as understanding that it's vital that she maintained a good relationship with her child's father, and if he called her at 10 o'clock and we're laid up, there are boundaries, but she may have to answer that call. Those type of commitments and understandings, nowhere near was I ready for. That's a completely different ball game.

Some of that uncertainty comes from continuing to gain confidence as a man, growing into manhood. It was my first time dealing with that and I'm just wondering, "Am I settling?" As a 23-year-old, I ain't even got going in life yet and I'm off into a situation with a woman with a 10-year-old? At this time, I'm thinking that I might be playing basketball for the next 10 years in multiple countries. Who's to say I won't meet another woman? I still don't want to tie myself down yet because this is only my second season. I'm just now getting used to traveling the world.

We kicked it the rest of my time in Qatar, but at the end of the day, we just weren't compatible. We weren't on that type of level. Jess came back to the U.S. in March 2018, and I returned in April after our season ended. A few weeks later, we spent our birthdays together in Miami. We're still friends, but it's not intimate like it was.

I shot in the 50-40-90 club in Qatar. What that means is 50 percent from the field, 40 percent from the three-point line, and 90 percent from the free throw line. That's an accomplishment. I was averaging around 21 points a game. We were a decent team. We weren't great. However, the American teammates built a good relationship with each other and we're all still friends to this day. One of them is now a basketball coach at the University of Oregon. And I'm still friends with some of the guys who live over there in Qatar.

After that season ended, I was like, "OK, what's next?" I want to go to the next level. My agent Dmitry had some connections through Octagon, as they are a very prominent agency. On their NBA side, they got clients like Steph Curry, Giannis Antetokounmpo, and a lot of household names. On their Europe side, they got big names overseas. After I got my film together, compiled all my stats, and finished out the season in April, Dmitry started working.

Meanwhile I'm back in Nashville living with my dad's mom. May, June, July, I still hadn't signed. I had just finished a good year. The league wasn't a strong league, but my confidence was at an all-time high. I'm back working out in the summertime. I'm feeling good. My agent's still trying to get me interest in different places. At this point I'm like, "I want to give it a shot."

Late that summer, Dmitry asked me, "What do you think about the NBA G League?" I knew about the G League, but I never really considered playing in it. All I'm hearing is the word NBA in it. I asked him, "What type of money are we looking to make?" I believe the G League pays you around $35,000 to $40,000 over a seven-month span. That's not bad. I'm like, "OK, well, let's entertain it." Dmitry said, "I think I can get you a workout with the

Oklahoma City Blue. I can't guarantee anything to come from it, but I can get you in front of the coaches."

When September came around, the Oklahoma City Blue invited four other guys and me to come in for a private workout. I had to purchase my own plane ticket but to me it was an investment. I checked into a cheap hotel nearby and got me a rental car. I'm kind of in awe. This is just a hell of an experience. Little did I know that this would be a blessing in disguise.

The Oklahoma City Blue is one of the very few G League teams located in the same city as its NBA team, in this case the Oklahoma City Thunder. Both facilities are right there together. I'm like, "Damn. We're working out at the Thunder's facility." As a kid, this is what you dream about. I remember sitting out there and taking pictures of the facility to send to my family: "Yo, this is real. I'm actually here."

When I walk in for the workout, the team is finished up with practice. In 2018, Carmelo Anthony had just left, and Paul George and Russell Westbrook were still in Oklahoma City. These are two superstars. The other four recruits and I are given a tour of the practice facility. We meet the private chefs. We see where the team parks. We watch some guys working out after practice. Right there, in the training room, is Russell Westbrook. He's an A-list celebrity. He had just had knee surgery. He comes out and introduces himself to us as if we don't already know who he is.

He was like, "Russell." In my mind I'm like, "Motherfucker, we know." But I'm like, "Darrius." We're all introducing ourselves and it was right then—it was like a light bulb just clicked. When I get in there and I meet him, it dawns on me that something is still missing inside me. That should have been a thrilling moment. Here I am getting ready to work out at the highest level possible in an NBA facility with all these people. For your whole life, you picture something being a certain way, and then you obtain it and it's like, "This is it?"

My fear of performing and my fear of meeting expectations went completely out the window. It's like how people tell you, "Man, these people are human and just like you." It sounds cliché but it's the truth. I told myself, "This is another day in the park. Go play basketball." With that being said, I killed the workout because my mindset was in a different place. I'm going at these guys. These are all high-major guys who played at big schools and I'm busting their ass. I'm scoring and playing good defense too.

Again, I wasn't that passionate or that overly thrilled about being in that environment, but I wasn't timid. I wasn't fearful. I wasn't afraid of messing up because in my mind it was like, "If I get out there and don't do well, so what?" I didn't have that feeling of pressure or think, "Oh, I've got to perform so I can come back here." This is when the process started to slowly transition into, I got to do more soul searching and figure out, who am I really doing this for? Is this really what I want to be doing?

Mark Daigneault, the head coach for the Oklahoma City Blue, and Matt McCall, my coach at UT Chattanooga, knew each other from coaching together at the University of Florida under Billy Donovan (who at this time was the head coach for the Oklahoma City Thunder). So, Coach Daigneault knew my background before I came, and he was aware that I played for his buddy in college. He's in the gym watching us and I can tell that I'm catching his eye. When the workout's over, the other four guys are getting ready to leave, but Coach Daigneault pulls me to the side. He said, "Tell me a little bit about your college journey."

After I did that, I stuffed a heck of a lot of gear in my rental car. Coach McCall texted me when I was en route to the airport and said, "I don't know what type of dinner you cooked for Mark and his staff, but he thinks the world of you. You must have put on a show. They are thrilled!" Mind you, this is the same coach that I was ready to be like, "Fuck him." It's the same guy. His words caught me off guard. I said, "Yeah, Coach, just playing with a free mind." In so many words, I also wanted to tell him, "I could have been doing this at Chatt but you just didn't give me a shot."

Then he said, "When Mark gets back to his office, he's got to look at a few things, but you'll be hearing from him." I didn't know if that meant I'm on the team, but at this point I'm feeling good. I called Dmitry to let him know how it all went. He said he would follow up with the team and do his due diligence.

About a week later, the director of operations for the Blue invited me to training camp with the team. This time, it's on their budget. They fly me there.

They put me in a nice hotel suite for my two weeks of training camp. We have a chef. I have a driver to get back and forth to practice. We're getting into the real deal. This is the big time. This is unheard of where I'm from. I had reached the highest tier of the sport. It don't get no bigger NBA. I had reached that plateau and it was still like an empty feeling. I told myself, "I'm going to ride this wave until it's done, and when it's done, it's done. I've accomplished everything that I wanted to accomplish with it."

I have a lot of friends who played in the NFL, so they gave me words of encouragement and wisdom going into training camp. They were very supportive, just letting me know to be myself. They'd say, "Go in there and play your game. It ain't nothing different than what you're used to. Don't let the name and the environment trick your mind or tell you something else." They were with me the whole path of the way.

At training camp, some of the Thunder players are in there with you. They have what you call a two-way, where a guy can play in the G League and the NBA. I'm meeting guys that I grew up watching, meaning they were McDonald's All-Americans when I was in middle school. Big time prospects and now they're my competitors. There's also politics when it comes to playing at that level. A lot of, "What school did you come from?" or "Where have you played?" or "How high are you ranked?" It's bullshit, but it carries weight.

For a typical day at training camp, we'd get to the facility early in the morning, and the chef would be preparing breakfast. You could do weights either before or after you ate. Then we'd have some downtime, but you had to be on the court by 10, ready to practice. A lot of times guys would eat their breakfast, get their workout in, and start getting shots up. When 10 o'clock hits, it's time to roll. Ain't no "It's 10 o'clock, so now you start stretching." No, no, no. Ain't no coach calling your phone to see where you are. No, no, no, no.

Practice would be from 10 to 12. Two hours of intense practice, followed by a film breakdown of what just happened in practice. That would last maybe 30 to 45 minutes. After that, lunch has already been prepared by the chef, so you eat and get your treatment if you need it. Then you're pretty much done for the day. You can come back and shoot later if you want to. Whatever you want to do, you've got the rest of the day to yourself. That was the routine every day. It's a system and you need to be handling your business and conducting yourself accordingly.

We had an inner-team scrimmage that Saturday to end training camp. Very competitive. It was only me and another guy who were there as prospects. Everybody else was returning, or they were new guys who had already signed their deal. I don't know if the two of us were there to fill in practice slots or if we even had a fair chance of making the team. I shot the ball fairly well but it was almost like the AAU days. I didn't do anything exceptional to set myself apart. Can I play at that level? Damn right, I know I can, because I held my own. But I'm 6'4". You got guys that are 6'7" or 6'8" playing my same position, doing what I'm doing. Which guy is more marketable?

After the scrimmage, we went out to Topgolf as a team and headed out to the club after that. We wanted to celebrate training camp and the two weeks of brotherhood that were created over training camp. Even for the guys who were going to get cut, it was bonding time. I had a blast. Sunday morning comes. I'm hungover because we was out kicking it. I get a text from the compliance guy about 8:30 a.m., saying "You got a meeting with Coach Mark at 10:15 in his office." I kind of knew what that was about, but then again, I didn't. This was at the end of October and the first game was scheduled for November 2, so the season's getting ready to crank up. I'm thinking, "I done made it this far. I'm probably on the team."

Coach kept it short and sweet. His pitch was, "This is always one of the hardest days just because it's not anything really you did wrong. It's a numbers game. Do I think you can perform at this level? Absolutely. Do I think there's some things that you may need to work on? Absolutely. But that's everybody, 1 through 12 on the team." Then he said, "I'm going to cut you."

That feeling of rejection came back, of being inadequate. Then again, I had to remind myself like, dude, you're defying odds. I wasn't angry. I respected what he said, but I still felt a slight sense of that child in me that was triggered by rejection. He told me, "I'm more than willing to help you any way I can. If another G League team wants to sign you, or if you need film for overseas, or whatever the case may be, I'm more than willing to help you in any way I can."

The compliance guy booked me for a flight home for the next morning. They flew me out of there faster than they got me.

When you get cut from an NBA G League team, any other NBA team has 10 days to claim you. If they choose not to, then you become a free agent and you can do whatever you want. My 10 days were up and nobody else was showing serious interest. So, I went back to play in Qatar in November. Because I had the NBA G League stamp on my résumé, I got paid a little more.

My attitude was like, "I just came from playing in the NBA G League. This ain't nothing." Then in January, in the middle of a game, I came down on a guy's foot and fractured my right ankle. Suddenly, eight weeks after I got cut from the G League, that injury ended my season. The contracts to play in Qatar are non-guaranteed. If you get cut or hurt, you don't get what you sign for. Your payment stops that day. They gave me the option to train in Qatar until I got better, but I wouldn't be getting paid. Or they said I could go home and rehab. If I'm not getting paid, I'm not staying out here! I went home in January 2019 and rehabbed with my trainer for a while, because I still had the intention of getting healthy and playing again the following season.

At this time, the nonprofit work started picking up. Before I left for the G League, two partners and I created a nonprofit called the WTE Institute, but we weren't off to a fast start. We were just doing a few community things here and there. When I came back from Qatar in 2019, that's when it really kicked in. We started hosting programs at the juvenile centers with young kids who were in custody. I felt it on my heart because I could imagine my own experiences as a kid.

I'd been chasing this vision that I had now accomplished, and then realized it ain't everything I thought it would be. It was burning in my heart to share that experience, so people could gain clarity and understanding that you should follow a dream because it's what you want to do, not because it's what people are putting on you. When I got hurt, people still tried to figure out like, "When are you going back to hoop?"

This is when I started therapy. I did 120 days. Four months, twice a week. The reason I say 120 days is because when you're not in the meetings, you're still going through the process because they give you homework. Man, it was tough. It was a dark road because I had to unlearn everything that I had learned to get to where I was trying to go. What that meant was getting to the root of my triggers, getting to the root of traumatic experiences, and holding people accountable for situations or experiences that I may have been faced with.

That was a much-needed process, but it wasn't an easy process. It was peeling back layers and layers of suppressed emotions and thoughts. These things can get covered up and suppressed by your job or your vices, and you don't take time to tune in to them. Before you know it, you make all your decisions based on these irrational emotions. Going through this process made it clearer than ever that basketball had served its purpose.

As a kid the NBA never really was the goal. The goal was always, "What can I do to change the environment of the people around me, of myself, my family, and the people around me?" Basketball was the outlet. However, the surrounding cast of family, friends, and peers portrayed their vision of what they wanted for me on me. I'd hear, "Boy, you keep on going, you going to go to the NBA, you going to be this, you going to be that." You allow that to almost become your identity because that's what people are constantly telling you. You feel like, "OK, this, what I'm supposed to be doing, chasing this basketball dream," but not really listening to your own voice. That's what I had got caught up in.

It wasn't until I went through these sessions of gaining self-awareness that I realized, "Dude, you've done more than enough. If you want to stop today, you've made history." That made walking away from the game an easy, peaceful decision. The more I went through this self-work and got more heavily engaged with the youth, it brought an internal smile and a feeling I can't really explain. Really helping somebody, impacting somebody in a way that is tangible. To me, that was way more fulfilling than ever scoring 30 points, 40 points, or more. That's when I knew it's time for a change in direction.

By the spring of 2019, I didn't have any interest to continue playing. I had zero interest in going out of the country to play for eight to ten months. I was in tune with what my purpose was. To get there, I relied on the same questions we used with the juveniles: Who am I? How do I know? And how do I reconcile with others? Now that I know who I am, how do I transition back into society as this new individual?

Based on my passion and purpose, this is when entrepreneurship took over. Again, the goal is to change the environment of yourself and the people around you. I said, "I've got to get in the position to where I can provide jobs for a lot of these young men that I'm trying to impact." I wanted to provide opportunities for a lot of these young men I'm trying to impact. I wanted to provide exposure for a lot of these young men I'm trying to impact. How do I do that?

I was telling my vision to one of my weight trainers at the gym, and he said, "There's a guy that works out in here. He's got a cleaning company. You might want to run your idea by him. He may have some different jobs that need help." That's how I met Gerald Jones. I set up a meeting with him and I let him know I'm in the nonprofit industry and what I wanted to achieve.

At the time, the NFL draft was coming to Nashville and Gerald had the contract to clean up the trash in the fan zone area. He asked me, "Can you put a crew together?" He basically gave me an assignment to manage a 10-man team for the entire draft weekend to fulfill this task. I wasn't even his employee yet. He wanted to see what I was about first. That's how I look at it now.

So, I did it. I went to Dismas House, which is the halfway house in Nashville for second-chance offenders fresh out of prison. I made a relationship with Dismas and was able to give two of their residents a job, then I put a 10-man crew together and I was able to manage it. I was like, "This is fire, but I don't really know this industry. I've never done anything like this."

After Gerald seeing I could do that, shortly after he pitched a supervisor role for me. He had a contract with three schools and needed somebody to oversee them. I knew it would put me back into the position of working for somebody, but I kind of had to do that, because if I'm going to be in this industry, I need to educate myself in this industry before I jump in it. I worked with Gerald for a year straight and learned what I thought I needed to know about a maintenance and cleaning company before I could do it myself.

After these schools let out for the day, we're the janitor. I went from being in an NBA facility with a A-list celebrity to pushing a mop bucket. In these schools, you're the bottom on the totem pole. You're the one that cleans up the piss and the trash. Nobody has respect for the janitors. Nobody. You can feel that disrespect and you experience with a lot of the school administration because what we do is so beneath them. I wanted to tell so many people about themselves and it was tempting at times. Yeah, I got a bachelor's degree too. You're not the only one. I'm pretty sure our salaries are probably the same. I'm not getting paid by the hour. If you want to roll out résumés, we can do that. Don't get me pushing this mop bucket confused. This is what I do, not who I am. For someone to view me in a sense of, "Oh, he's a peon...." Now this ain't that. I'm an intelligent, wise individual. I give respect, and I demand the same thing in return.

It was a humbling experience for me because I'm somebody. For the last eight years of my life, I was viewed on a pedestal. I come from that mentality, and to be put in this position gave me a different perspective of the population that I was going to be serving, and it gave me a better understanding of reality. I had to go through those interactions, because if this is a population I want to serve, I got to be able to relate to what they're dealing with. People out here got it rough.

Nobody understood why I was doing that, even my own mama. From the outside looking in, here's a man who was just at the NBA training camp and now he wants to be a janitor. Nobody understood, but the picture was way bigger than that. I needed to know the intels of completing the task. Looking back, I wouldn't change that experience for anything in the world. With that being said, it was a lonely journey because nobody really understood what I was trying to do.

I still lived with grandma at the time, but I bought my first house a year later. At this time, me and my mom are still reconciling our relationship. She and her husband are doing their thing and I went through the home-buying process without her. I didn't let her know I had got a house until I was getting ready to close. Then I finally told her. This was all something new for her. She had never bought a home, so that was another generational curse broken.

Now people's heads are kind of turned, like, "He must've got some money put up from overseas." People are starting to come around a little bit, but I'm still grinding in these schools, pushing the mop buckets around.

When Covid hit in the spring of 2020, I stopped working with Gerald and started my own maintenance company. I had watched how Gerald did certain things and he taught me how to bid on contracts. When I walk into a building, looking to see how I'm going to charge, what am I looking for? What do I need to be seeing? I had to learn all that. At this point I was confident.

To this day, I still try to offer jobs to the youth that I'm serving. That's the goal. Whenever I can, I try to bring them along as much as possible. Conversations are different now too. The respect for the janitor is different when you find out the janitor owns the company. Now the people in my life who didn't really understand the big picture are acting as if they could see the vision the whole time. I've still got a facility maintenance company and a few other business endeavors that I'm involved in, including owning real estate. I'm just trying to obtain what I can to create more resources and opportunities for others. I might kid and I might joke, but I do not play!

Soon after I started my company, public speaking opportunities started to come together. People wanted to hear my story. They wanted to hear about the journey. At the end of Chapter One, I told you I was on a mission to rebrand my family. When I say "family," obviously it's my bloodline, but most importantly, it's also those who are products of lower-income, marginalized communities. I can't change the world. That's not my plan. With every young adult I meet, my plan is to give them another perspective on how they may view the world. If I can impact that perspective and their mindset, the rest is a domino effect. Starting right there with the mind.

When I decided to stop playing basketball, I turned down the money so that I could pursue my passion and I ended up with both. I have nothing but gratitude for the game of basketball, and zero regret about walking away. I thoroughly enjoy the bumps and grinds of what I'm doing now. It's not easy. Before I go to bed, I typically know what I got to get up and do the next morning. It can be inconsistent, but a lot of times I will get up and do some type of workout. Maybe read a small passage or listen to a podcast. Very rarely do I get off to a slow start to where I'm just lounging around until two in the afternoon. No, no, no. That's even true on the weekends, unless I had a long night, which my body still naturally wakes up on its own. I'm still very tired from the long nights and early mornings, but I'm building something. I'm walking with that passion and that purpose along this journey. Never do I wake up and say, "Damn I wish I would have...."

Instead, I think, "How can we win today?" I wake up passionate, more times than not. I've gotten better at mastering the decision of not letting yesterday affect today. We don't have bad days. We have bad moments. If something occurs that I'm unhappy with, I deal with it and move on accordingly. I may have to revisit it, but I don't let it linger into the next thing that I'm doing. That helps me to continue to strive forward, to take the lesson from it and keep going.

All of life's lessons and your journey will prepare you for the things that are in store ahead of you. It is essential for us to face our fears and adversity as it is the prerequisite for reaching the next levels in life. In reality the real game actually takes place before the game. It's all in our preparation that will determine the outcome of anything we do in life. The right result will follow. Just be sure to prepare yourself to the best of your ability day by day, step by step!

www.ingramcontent.com/pod-product-compliance
Lightning Source LLC
LaVergne TN
LVHW042253070526
838201LV00106B/306/J